GUIDE TO TEACHING A LANGUAGE ARTS CURRICULUM FOR HIGH-ABILITY LEARNERS

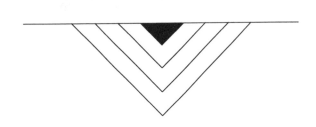

The College of William and Mary
School of Education
Center for Gifted Education
Williamsburg, VA 23187-8795

GUIDE TO TEACHING A LANGUAGE ARTS CURRICULUM FOR HIGH-ABILITY LEARNERS

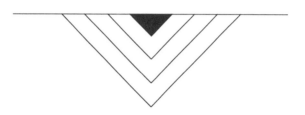

The College of William and Mary
School of Education
Center for Gifted Education
Williamsburg, VA 23187-8795

Center for Gifted Education Staff:
Project Director: Dr. Joyce VanTassel-Baska
Project Manager: Dana T. Johnson
Project Consultants: Linda Neal Boyce, Catherine A. Little

Funded by the Jacob K. Javits Program, United States Department of Education, under a subcontract from Washington-Saratoga-Warren-Hamilton-Essex BOCES, Saratoga Springs, New York.

KENDALL/HUNT PUBLISHING COMPANY
4050 Westmark Drive   Dubuque, Iowa 52002

Copyright © 1999 by Center for Gifted Education

ISBN 0-7872-5349-9

Printed in the United States of America
10 9 8 7 6 5 4 3 2

Contents

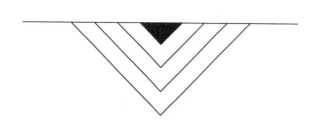

SECTION

I

INTRODUCTION
TO THE
WILLIAM AND MARY
CENTER FOR
GIFTED EDUCATION UNITS

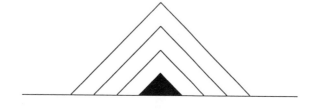

▼ A. Utilization of Unit Materials

What is the William and Mary Center for Gifted Education Language Arts curriculum?

The William and Mary language arts curriculum is an integrated program of study that emphasizes all four strands of language arts instruction: literature, writing, oral communication, and language study. Moreover, because the program is designed for high-ability learners, there is a strong emphasis on higher level thinking and concept development within the language arts and across to other disciplines. The program may be implemented as a core language arts experience and supplemented as necessary with other materials. The units cover a range or grade levels, encompassing elementary through high school. Each unit represents a semester of work.

How do the units relate to curriculum reform?

The William and Mary units were developed using appropriate curriculum dimensions for high-ability students but also using design features of curriculum reform. Specifically, the units employ the following emphases:

- ▼ *Meaning-based*—emphasizing depth over breadth, concepts over facts, and grounded in real world issues and problems that students of today care about or need to understand.

- ▼ *Higher order thinking*—treating thinking skills as integral to all content areas and providing students with opportunities to demonstrate their understanding of them through strategies such as concept mapping, persuasive writing, and conducting research.

- ▼ *Intra- and interdisciplinary connections*—using overarching concepts, issues, and themes as the organizers for making connections between areas of study.

- ▼ *Metacognition*—reflecting on one's own learning processes and consciously planning, monitoring, and assessing learning for efficient and effective use of time and resources.

- ▼ *Habits of mind*—cultivating modes of thinking that resemble those of professionals in various fields with respect to skills, predispositions, and attitudes.

- ▼ *Active learning and problem-solving*—putting students in charge of their own learning—finding out what they know, what they don't know, and what they need to know.

- ▼ *Concept-based*—organizing activities around a broad, interdisciplinary concept that promotes deep thinking and substantive connections within and across disciplines.

- ▼ *Multiculturalism and globalism*—recognizing that America is not the center of the universe, that other countries and cultures have made significant contributions to the progress of humankind in many areas. Moreover, curriculum should reflect in an equitable way the contributions of minority groups comprising America today through activities, strategies, and materials.

- ▼ *Technology-relevant*—using various new technologies as tools for the learning process, from doing library research via CD-ROM and the Internet, to composing at the word processor, to communicating with students across the world by e-mail.

▼ *Learner outcomes of significance*—setting expectations for learning segments at targeted grade levels that reflect the priorities of the new curriculum for being broad-based, conceptual, and relevant to real world application.

▼ *Authentic assessment*—tapping into what students know as a result of meaningful instruction, using approaches such as portfolios and performance-based activities.

What are the goals of the curriculum?

The goals of each of the language arts learning units are as follows:

▼ To develop analytical and interpretive skills in literature.

▼ To develop persuasive writing skills.

▼ To develop linguistic competency.

▼ To develop listening/oral communication skills.

▼ To develop reasoning skills in the language arts.

▼ To understand the concept of change.

How should teachers use the units?

The William and Mary Center for Gifted Education language arts units were developed to be used as a semester-long core language arts curriculum in various classroom settings. The curriculum has been designed for use with high-ability learners but has been used successfully with less able students if reading selections are differentiated according to reading level.

Each unit is organized around the Integrated Curriculum Model (ICM) that is carefully mapped on specific lessons. To honor this integrated approach, teachers need to be flexible in the actual number of sessions that students may need in order to work through the unit. What is important is that all lessons are taught in some depth to ensure that the major goals and unit outcomes are sufficiently addressed.

Anatomy of a Language Arts Unit

Each unit contains the following sections for easy reference:

▼ *Curriculum framework:* The set of unit goals and outcomes is stated for easy reference.

▼ *Lesson plans:* A set of 24 lesson plans is presented, each with considerations for instructional purpose, materials needed, activities, questions, and assessment ideas.

▼ *Assessment:* Assessment approaches in the unit include pre-post reading and writing performance tasks, pre-post grammar test, writing assessments, research presentation assessments, a critical thinking assessment and portfolio work to be collected and assessed in each lesson, and a final assessment measuring major objectives of the unit.

▼ *References:* The set of specific references that are useful for implementing the unit may be found at the end of the unit.

Language Arts Teaching Strategies

All of the units emphasize the following strategies:

▼ **Questions:** Questions are organized to address important aspects of unit learning. They focus on understanding change, on the elements of reasoning, and on literary response and interpretation. Thus, typically, questions are grouped within lessons according to those designations as in the following example:

Sample Question Set
(Based on the short story "Charles")

Literary Response and Interpretation Questions

▼ *Why does Laurie need Charles?*

▼ *What do you think the main idea of the story is? Provide evidence from the story to support your point of view.*

▼ *What does the phrase "elaborately casual" mean in the third paragraph of the story? How does the mother really feel? How do you know?*

▼ *Why does Laurie never talk about what he himself did at school? What clues do you have about Charles's identity during the story?*

▼ *Why are Laurie's parents so anxious to meet Charles's mother?*

▼ *What does Laurie's father mean when he says, "I don't see how they could hold a PTA meeting without Charles's mother"?*

▼ *How effective was the ending of the story? Explain your response.*

▼ *The story reports what happened each day at Laurie's house as he described Charles's behavior. What do you think conversations were like at the other kinder-gartners' houses? Laurie's mother went to the meeting anxious to meet Charles's mother. What might the other mothers have been thinking? How do you think Laurie's mother's perceptions of the other mothers changed after she spoke to the teacher?*

▼ *What might be another title for this story? Give several reasons for your response.*

Reasoning Questions

▼ *Who is Charles? Give **evidence** from the story to support your opinion.*

▼ *What **point of view** do Laurie's parents have about Charles?*

▼ *What can you **infer** about Laurie's feelings about his experiences, based on events in the story? Give **evidence** from the story for your ideas.*

▼ *What can you **infer** about Laurie's adjustment to kindergarten from his teacher's comment "We had a little trouble adjusting, the first week or so, but now he's a fine little helper. With occasional lapses, of course."*

Change Questions

▼ *How does Charles's behavior **change** in the story? Why does it change?*

▼ *How do the generalizations about **change** relate to this story?*

▼ **Discussion:** A major emphasis is recommended on the use of discussion in the language arts classroom. Thinking is promoted best through discourse, so such conversation is important. Both small groups and the whole class of learners need to engage in frequent discussions about their work. The questioning model used in the units is the way to ensure a focused discussion lesson. However, teachers are also encouraged to use the graphic organizers such as the literature web, Venn diagrams, change matrices, and other such tools to aid discussion as well.

▼ **Metacognition:** Metacognition is treated in the units through several approaches. The research project provides an opportunity for students to plan, monitor, and assess their progress on a given issue. Moreover, response journals allow students to reflect on their learning experiences after selected lessons.

▼ **Concept teaching:** The teaching of the concept of change is systematically encouraged in the unit through specific lessons. In addition, teachers are encouraged to post the generalizations about change in the classroom and to have students extemporaneously comment on how change is relevant as they go through the unit.

▼ **Higher level thinking:** The deliberate use of the Paul model of reasoning provides a way for the units to focus on higher level thinking. Teachers may use the model in all aspects of unit implementation.

▼ **Communication skills:** The program stresses the equal importance of written and oral communication skills. Activities that promote the use of these skills are embedded throughout the units of study.

Grouping

The units have been implemented in a variety of grouping settings, including heterogeneous classrooms, pull-out programs, and self-contained gifted classes. Based on our feedback from national pilots, we suggest that school districts employ their existing grouping approach to teach the unit the first time. Based on individual district results from the first year of implementation, decisions about regrouping procedures may be explored.

Use with Other Language Arts Resources

The use of the language arts units as a core resource works well with other existing supplementary language arts materials, particularly the following:

▼ *Junior Great Books*
▼ *Word within a Word*
▼ *The Magic Lens*
▼ *Writing 2000* and the *Johns Hopkins University Writing Workshop Model*
▼ *Touchpebbles* and *Touchstones* materials
▼ Selected grammar, spelling, and usage resources

See Part VI for reference information on these resources.

Evaluating Student Progress

Teachers are encouraged to evaluate student progress through multiple means, including performance-based activities, portfolios of student work, and end of unit assessment forms. Specific assessment guidelines are contained within the units. National data are available for comparison purposes regarding student gains in literary analysis and interpretation, persuasive writing, and linguistic competency by unit.

Scope and Sequence

The definitional structure of scope and sequence may be found in the curriculum work of VanTassel-Baska (1992). Scope refers to the extensiveness of the curriculum experiences across a predetermined period of time. The determination of scope hinges on the value attached to what is to be taught. For purposes of the William and Mary Center for Gifted Education curriculum, the scope of the curriculum is limited to core concepts and units of study usable for 9–18 weeks of full-time instruction. Sequence refers to the order in which the desired curriculum experiences will be taught and learned. For purposes of this curriculum, the order was established around student progression of knowledge, skills, and concepts from grades 2 through 11. Individual units have been targeted for use at specific grade level clusters over the span of years. The following list illustrates how the units allow students to progress over the years the units are used:

1. Concept learning becomes more advanced as new and more complex applications are made in each succeeding unit.
2. Reasoning becomes more complex as students apply more aspects of the Paul model in their work.
3. The choice of literature becomes more advanced in each unit.
4. Applications in all the language arts areas become more in-depth, complex, and rigorous.

Many school districts choose to use a series of the language arts units across elementary and middle school years. Use of different units across grade levels is encouraged to provide multiple applications of the concept of change, the use of the reasoning process, and the enhancement of language arts skills.

The following example provides one illustration of sequencing the units for use with gifted learners over time in the Hanover County, Virginia school system. The district employs a heterogeneous classroom delivery model in which gifted students are cluster grouped in order to receive instruction in the language arts units.

Grade Level	Unit Title
2–3	*Journeys and Destinations*
4	*Patterns of Change*
5	*Literary Reflections*
6	*Autobiographies*
7	*Persuasion*
8	*The 1940s: A Decade of Change*
9	*Threads of Change*

▼ B. Differentiation for High-Ability Learners

The William and Mary Center for Gifted Education language arts curriculum was developed with an eye to characteristics and needs of high-ability learners. The following chart illustrates this relationship:

High-Ability Learner Characteristics	Corresponding Emphases in the Curriculum
Advanced reading ability	Corresponding rich, complex literature selected
Advanced vocabulary	Corresponding emphasis on vocabulary development
Abstract reasoning skills	Emphasis on high level reasoning in discussion of literature, writing assignments, and oral presentations
Ability to make connections	Thematic organization of curriculum
Power of concentration	Emphasis on analysis and interpretation of literature Emphasis on long-term projects and meaningful homework
Concern for moral and ethical issues	Research on issues of significance
Emotional sensitivity	Opportunities for personal response to literature and language
Ability to generate original ideas	Emphasis on generative project work

The unit contains advanced reading selections and presents challenging activities at increased levels of complexity, all essential curriculum elements for high-ability learners. Specific adaptations made throughout the unit to accommodate these learners include the following:

1. The literature selected for the unit meets the specific criteria for high-ability learners suggested by Baskin and Harris (1980). A detailed description of these criteria follows:

   ▼ The language used in books for the gifted should be rich, varied, precise, complex, and exciting, for language is the instrument for the reception and expression of thought.

   ▼ Books should be chosen with an eye to their open-endedness, their capacity to inspire contemplative behavior, such as through techniques of judging time sequences, shifting narrators, and unusual speech patterns of characters.

   ▼ Books for the gifted should be complex enough to allow interpretive and evaluative behaviors to be elicited from readers.

   ▼ Books for the gifted should help them build problem-solving skills and develop methods of productive thinking.

   ▼ Books should provide characters as role models for emulation.

   ▼ Books should be broad-based in form, from picture books, to folktale and myths, to nonfiction, to biography, to poetry, to fiction.

2. The inclusion of high quality multicultural literature adds another dimension of complexity. Criteria for the selection of this literature, based on Miller-Lachmann (1992), follows:

    ▼ General accuracy: Works should adhere to high standards of scholarship and authentic portrayal of thoughts and emotions.

    ▼ Avoidance of stereotypes: Stereotyping occurs when an author assigns general characteristics to a group rather than exploring its members' diversity and individuality.

    ▼ Language: Language issues include appropriateness to age group, up-to-date terminology, avoidance of loaded words, and authentic use of dialect.

    ▼ Attention to author's perspective: Perspective includes the author's mind-set, point of view, experience, and values.

    ▼ Currency of facts and interpretation: Copyright date alone does not assure recent information.

    ▼ Concept of audience: Some books appeal to general audiences while others consider issues about heritage and cultural values that have special appeal to members of a specific group. The challenge is for authors to develop the reader's empathy.

    ▼ Integration of cultural information: Cultural information must be presented in a manner consistent with the flow of the story.

    ▼ Balance and multidimensionality: Books range from presenting an "objective" perspective, which may contain subtle biases, to those stating a particular viewpoint. Readers should have opportunities to see the multidimensionality of characters and cultures.

    ▼ Illustrations: Issues that relate to text also apply to illustrations: for instance, illustrations must be accurate and up-to-date and without stereotypes.

3. The inquiry model of discussion moves students from initial reactions to analysis and interpretation of a reading or speech. It invites students to consider multiple perspectives.

4. Vocabulary study in the units extends well beyond definitions. It models the study of challenging words including investigation of etymology, antonyms, synonyms, and related words.

5. Consideration of important issues is treated at several levels of sophistication. Individual points of view are supported and argued through techniques of persuasion. Students are also required to consider and address other points of view.

6. Interdisciplinary connections are made in the units not only by integrating the language arts with the "sister" arts of music and visual arts but also by addressing changes in social, cultural, economic, and political aspects of various societies.

7. Use of a critical thinking model consistently encourages students to focus on the application of important elements of reasoning in their study of literature.

▼ C. Research Evidence of Effectiveness

The language arts units were developed as a part of a Javits grant from the United States Department of Education awarded to BOCES of Saratoga Springs, New York, and subcontracted to the Center for Gifted Education at the College of William and Mary in Virginia. Part of the curriculum development process has included the piloting of the units in classrooms around the nation and the collection of data on student achievement within each unit. Currently, the faculty, staff, and graduate students of the Center for Gifted Education are engaged in a series of studies that are examining aspects of the implementation of the curriculum and its underlying pedagogy in schools. These studies may be clustered around the following categories:

Curriculum Effectiveness Studies

We are engaged in a series of curriculum effectiveness studies that are examining the curriculum impact by unit, by developmental level (primary, intermediate, and middle school), by classrooms over time (implementation of three or more units), and by teachers over time (three year implementations). Moreover, the Center is also conducting replications of basic student impact studies at new sites (VanTassel-Baska, Hughes, Johnson, Boyce, and Hall, 1997).

Classroom Implementation Studies

We also are interested in understanding how the curriculum works on a day-to-day basis at the classroom level. Thus, we are exploring teacher behaviors, use of specific strategies and embedded assessments (non-usable material, modifications, and extensions), and classroom interaction processes (Burruss, 1997).

Special Population Studies

We also wish to understand the impact of the curriculum on special populations of students, especially disadvantaged and minority students. Two questions of interest are 1) how effective is the curriculum with disadvantaged and minority students? and 2) are the effects differential or comparable to those found with more advantaged populations? Comparison of student outcome effects are also of interest with other special populations. One dissertation study, for example, is focusing on the teaching of persuasive writing through the use of the Paul model to gifted, learning disabled, and average students (Hughes, in preparation).

Classroom and School Studies of Change

Finally, we have an interest in studying how curriculum influences school change and reform. Consequently, we are studying teacher use of the units over three years and more to determine collective impacts on school and district use over time (VanTassel-Baska, Avery, Little, and Hughes, in press). We are specifically interested in how institutionalized the curriculum becomes in selected districts as judged by its presence in district policies, its classroom utility, and its perception by relevant stakeholders, such as parents, students, and teachers.

Findings

In the area of language arts, we have found significant and impressive gains in literature, persuasive writing, and linguistic competency for experimental classes using the curriculum (VanTassel-Baska, Johnson, Hughes, and Boyce, 1996). Individual content analyses reveal different patterns of growth, however. Overall findings led to follow-up implementation studies and new questions. Why, for example, is there less growth in literary analysis and interpretation than writing for the majority of learners? Several hypotheses emerged around this question. One is that the curriculum units have a stronger emphasis on teaching the persuasive writing model directly than they do in teaching literary analysis. A second hypothesis is that the assessment of literary analysis and interpretation may not be taught to students as a rubric for self-assessment as is the case for writing. A third hypothesis, also to be entertained, focuses on the possibility of uneven implementation of the units, with more emphasis placed on persuasive writing.

In schools, we have found extensive evidence of institutionalizing of the curriculum with many constituent groups voicing strong support for its impact. Teachers remarked that the units helped students look for the big picture instead of just memorizing a lot of isolated information and that they promoted teacher learning as well. Several administrators noted that teachers have learned to draw back and be coaches, letting kids hit or miss the mark. Teachers noted that after using more than one unit, students began to demonstrate improvements in habits of mind, writing and self-reflection skills, and ability to work cooperatively in groups.

Parents cited the benefits of the units' carryover into the home. One parent noted: "When my child hears a speaker, he starts to critique what is being said and how things are interrelated." Another parent related: "This notion of having three arguments has now permeated our life. We wanted to go bowling and my son kept saying 'elaborate'." Students agreed that the gifted materials keep their minds working, and one perceptive young man observed: "We get smarter as the units get harder."

The use of high-powered curriculum materials designed with the needs of high-ability learners and the new curriculum reform paradigm in mind appears to result in greater learning on dimensions important to both language arts educators and educators of high-ability learners.

▼ D. TEACHER EDUCATION

Training workshops sponsored through the Center for Gifted Education provide teachers with competency in implementing the core strategies of the unit as well as informal tips for teaching various strands in the unit. We also recommend that teachers using the unit subscribe to our free listserv, where they can communicate with other teachers regarding specific implementation issues. Visit the Center's web site at *www.wm.edu/education/gifted.html* for more information on subscribing to the listserv.

For the past five years, the Center for Gifted Education has offered language arts curriculum institutes at The College of William and Mary and inservice workshops for teachers and administrators throughout the United States. The language arts curriculum inservice programs were designed to enable participants to relate state language arts frameworks to national standards and to the William and Mary Center for Gifted Education language arts units modeled on these standards, to select appropriate language arts materials for high-ability learners, to employ successful instructional strategies in language arts teaching, and to implement the language arts units in the classroom. To date, over 3,000 educators throughout the United States and in 15 international sites have participated in the institutes.

Based on these experiences, we recommend minimally a two-day training session for all teachers using the units. Workshops are generally comprised of these core segments:

1. Overview of Language Arts Curriculum
2. Teaching Concepts
3. Teaching the Paul Model of Reasoning
4. Using Literature Webs, Vocabulary Webs, and Venn Diagrams to Analyze Literature
5. Teaching Persuasive Writing
6. Using Debate
7. Teaching Research
8. Implementing a Specific Unit of Study
9. Authentic Assessment in the Language Arts Classroom
10. Alignment with State Standards

As a result of such curriculum development and teacher training efforts, the language arts units have been employed successfully over the past five years as a way of promoting the learning of high-ability and gifted students. They have provided an important catalyst for promoting the synergistic aspects of new learning principles as well as enhancing the elements of curriculum for these learners—one that is interdisciplinary, one that is challenging and engaging, and one that promotes generative work.

▼ E. BIBLIOGRAPHY

Baskin, B. H., & Harris, K. H. (1980). *Books for the gifted child*. New York: Bowker.

Burruss, J. D. (1997, April). Walking the talk: Implementation decisions made by teachers. Paper presented at the American Educational Research Association (AERA), Chicago, IL.

Hughes, C. (in preparation). A study of gifted, learning disabled, and average learners in the teaching of thinking through persuasive writing. Dissertation in progress.

Miller-Lachmann, L. (1992). *Our family, our friends, our world: An annotated guide to significant multicultural books for children and teenagers*. New Providence, NJ: Bowker.

VanTassel-Baska, J. (1992). *Planning effective curriculum for the gifted*. Denver, CO: Love Publishing.

VanTassel-Baska, J. (1993). Linking curriculum development of the gifted to school reform and restructuring. *Gifted Child Today, 16*(4), 34–39.

VanTassel-Baska, J. (1993). The development of academic talent. *Journal of the California Association of the Gifted, 23*(4), 14–21.

VanTassel-Baska, J. (1993). The national curriculum development projects for high ability learners: Key issues and findings. In N. Colangelo, S. G. Assouline, & D. L. Ambroson, *Talent development Volume II* (pp. 19–38). Dayton, OH: Ohio Psychology Press.

VanTassel-Baska, J. (1994). *Comprehensive curriculum for gifted learners* (2nd ed). Boston: Allyn & Bacon.

VanTassel-Baska, J. (1994). Development and assessment of integrated curriculum: A worthy challenge. *Quest, 5* (2), 1–6.

VanTassel-Baska, J. (1994). Findings from the national curriculum projects in science and language arts. In S. Assouline and N. Colangelo (Eds.), *Talent Development, Proceedings from the Wallace Symposium on Research in Gifted Education* (pp. 1–28). Ames, IA: University of Iowa.

VanTassel-Baska, J. (1995). Key features of successful science and mathematics educational reform initiatives. *Proceedings from Making It Happen: First in the World of Science and Mathematics Education*. Washington, DC: Executive Office of the President.

VanTassel-Baska, J. (1995). The development of talent through curriculum. *Roeper Review, 18,* 98–102.

VanTassel-Baska, J., Avery, L. D., Little, C. A., & Hughes, C. E. (in press). An evaluation of the implementation of curriculum innovation: The impact of the William and Mary units on schools. *Journal for the Education of the Gifted*.

VanTassel-Baska, J., Hughes, C. E., Johnson, D. T., Boyce, L. N., & Hall, D. R. (1997, April). Language arts curriculum effectiveness study: Results of a curriculum developed for high-ability students. Paper presented at the American Educational Research Association (AERA), Chicago, IL.

VanTassel-Baska, J., Johnson, D., Hughes, C., & Boyce, L. N. (1996). A study of language arts curriculum effectiveness with gifted learners. *Journal for the Education of the Gifted, 19,* 461–480.

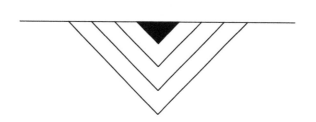

SECTION

II

CURRICULUM FRAMEWORK

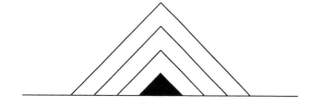

▼ A. The William and Mary Center for Gifted Education Curriculum Framework

The curriculum framework for developing the language arts units for high-ability learners is based on three major types of learner outcomes: concept outcomes organized around the theme of *change*, content outcomes organized around the four strands of the language arts (literature, writing, oral communication, and language study), and process outcomes organized around the elements of reasoning. Each set of outcomes guided the development of the units such that most lesson plans reflect an emphasis on each type of outcome. Figure 1 portrays this idea graphically.

Figure 1: Emphasis of Learner Outcomes on Unit Development

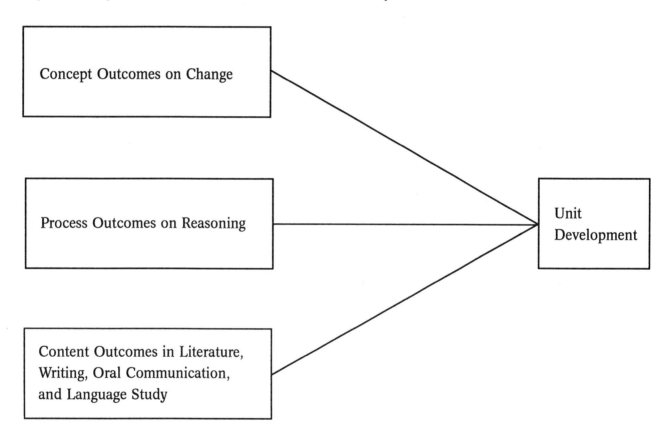

The diagram on the following page (Figure 2) represents the relationship of learner outcomes and teaching strategies employed in the language arts framework and underlying units of study. The conceptual structure of learner outcomes on the left provides the basis for the specific teaching strategies to be employed with students on the right. The units are centered on literature selections which provide the source for the conceptual outcomes to be explored and the catalyst for the learning strategies to be employed.

Figure 2: Constructing Meaning through Inquiry

What students need to understand   What teachers need to do with students

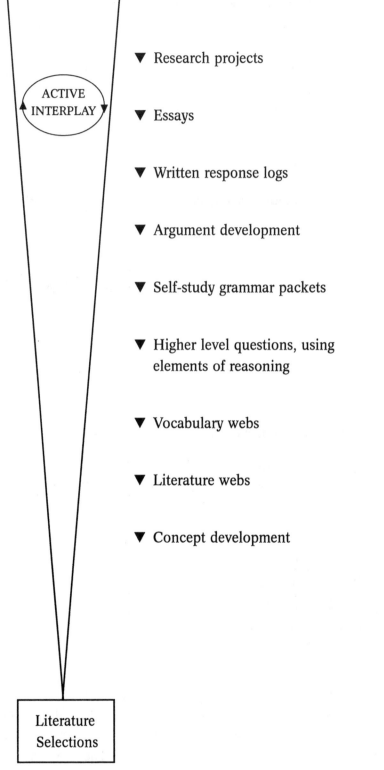

CHANGE
1. pervasive
2. linked to time
3. perceived as systematic or random
4. represents growth and development
   or regression and decay
5. occurs according to natural order or
   imposed by individuals or groups

ELEMENTS OF REASONING
1. purpose, goal, endview
2. issue of significance
3. point of view
4. assumptions
5. concept mastery
6. evidence
7. inferences
8. implications and consequences

LITERATURE
1. analysis
2. interpretation

WRITING
1. developing a significant issue
2. providing supporting evidence
3. synthesizing a conclusion
4. revising based on self, peer, and
   teacher review

SPEAKING AND LISTENING
1. evaluative listening
2. elements of persuasion
3. argument formulation
4. oral presentation

LINGUISTIC COMPETENCY
1. form of words
2. function of words
3. vocabulary
4. usage

ACTIVE INTERPLAY

▼ Research projects

▼ Essays

▼ Written response logs

▼ Argument development

▼ Self-study grammar packets

▼ Higher level questions, using
  elements of reasoning

▼ Vocabulary webs

▼ Literature webs

▼ Concept development

Literature
Selections

Adapted from Novak, J. D., & Gowin, D. B. (1984). *Learning how to learn.* New York: Cambridge University Press.

Learner Outcomes: Concept Dimension

The concept of change was selected for unit development based on its ease of application to various areas of the language arts as well as to other areas of study. Integral to understanding this concept are a set of generalizations derived from extensive reading on the concept in philosophy, sociology, and science. (See Appendix in this section for concept paper on change.) The generalizations are listed below:

▼ Change is pervasive.
▼ Change is linked to time.
▼ Change may be perceived as systematic or random.
▼ Change may represent growth and development or regression and decay.
▼ Change may occur according to natural order or be imposed by individuals or groups.

These generalizations have been converted into generic concept outcome statements for use in the units:

Students will be able to . . .

A. Understand that change is pervasive.
B. Illustrate the variability of change based on time.
C. Categorize types of change, given several examples.
D. Interpret change in selected works as progressive or regressive.
E. Demonstrate the change process at work in a piece of literature.
F. Analyze social and individual change in a given piece of literature.

Specific applications of these outcomes have been developed for the units of study:

1. The generalizations about change are used as one basis for literature discussion.
2. Vocabulary webs encourage students to understand how words have changed over time.
3. Selected writing assignments address the concept.
4. Emphasis on the writing process, oral communication, and research illustrate the concept of change as a process of individual learning.
5. Metacognition is emphasized as a change strategy for learning.
6. Culminating unit experiences trace the concept of change across time periods, cultures, and pieces of literature.

Learner Outcomes: Content Dimension

Content outcomes based on the key strands in language arts have been developed for the units. Outcome statements have been derived from broad goals for reading/literature, writing, language study, and oral communication. These outcome statements frame important bases for teaching and learning in the unit. The goals and learner outcomes developed are listed on the next page:

GOAL 1: To develop analytical and interpretive skills in literature.

Students will be able to . . .

    A. Describe what a selected literary passage means.

    B. Cite similarities and differences in meaning among selected works of literature.

    C. Make inferences based on information in given passages.

    D. Create a title for a reading selection and provide a rationale to justify it.

Specific applications of these outcomes have been developed for the curriculum units:

1. Pre- and post-assessments on literary analysis and interpretation are embedded in the unit.

2. Literature webs and other graphic organizers are used to promote literature understanding and response.

3. Response journals and logs are used to link literature to writing in the immediacy of the classroom discussion.

4. Specific study of vocabulary and language embedded in key selections of literature enhances literary understanding.

5. Each selected literary piece is used in a shared inquiry model of discussion that focuses students' construction of meaning based on their reading.

GOAL 2: To develop persuasive writing skills.

Students will be able to . . .

    A. Develop a written persuasive paragraph (thesis statement, supporting reasons, and conclusion), given a topic.

    B. Complete various pieces of writing using a three-phase revision process based on peer review, teacher feedback, and self-evaluation.

Specific applications of these outcomes have been developed for the curriculum units:

1. Pre- and post-assessments for writing using an argument model are embedded in the unit.

2. Students write expository paragraphs and essays using the persuasive writing model throughout the unit.

3. Students engage in the writing process approach.

4. Students develop at least one issue of significance in written form.

5. Students use concept maps to organize their thinking prior to writing.

6. Assessment of written work includes peer, self, and teacher evaluation.

GOAL 3: To develop linguistic competency.

Students will be able to . . .

    A. Develop vocabulary power commensurate with reading.

    B. Apply standard English usage in written and oral contexts.

    C. Evaluate effective use of words, sentences, and paragraphs in context.

Specific applications of these outcomes have been developed for the curriculum units:

1. Vocabulary webs are used to study the etymology, meaning, and relationships of words in literature. The webs promote increased word power and facilitate vocabulary analysis.

2. Revision and editing of written work give students opportunities to demonstrate and refine effective use of language.

3. Self-assessment and peer-assessment instruments provide opportunities to evaluate the use of language, vocabulary, and grammar.

GOAL 4: To develop listening/oral communication skills.

Students will be able to . . .

    A. Organize oral presentations.

    B. Evaluate an oral presentation, given a rubric of specific criteria.

Specific applications of these outcomes have been developed for the curriculum units:

1. The inquiry-based discussion model promotes active listening and expression of ideas.

2. Opportunities for oral presentations enhance communication skill.

3. Critical listening experiences are provided through guest and peer presentations.

4. Self-assessment and peer-assessment instruments provide opportunities to evaluate oral communication and elements of persuasion.

Learner Outcomes: Process Dimension

Just as the units promote a thematic or conceptual orientation in the teaching of language arts, they also emphasize a strong process orientation toward thinking and reasoning. Based on recent work in teaching critical thinking (Paul, 1992), the units focus on selected elements of reasoning for the teaching of reading, writing, speaking, and listening skills. Virtually all modes of communication involve these elements. The chart on the next page illustrates the elements of reasoning, with specific applications and assessment criteria related to the language arts curriculum.

Elements of Reasoning	Application Questions	Criteria for Assessment
1. Purpose, goal, or end view (e.g., does the student have a purpose—is it stated orally or in writing?)	What is the author's purpose in_____? What is the purpose of your essay (speech)?	Clarity, significance, realism, and consistency
2. Issue of significance, question at issue, or problem to be solved (e.g., can the student frame anissue—in writing, in debating, etc.?)	What is the central problem for the characters in the story? What is the major issue at stake?	Clarity in problem/issue formulation
3. Point of view (e.g., can a student formulate a consistent point of view and represent multiple points of view fairly?)	What is the author's point of view? What is your perspective on ____? Why?	Clarity and consistency (broad, flexible, fair)
4. Assumptions (e.g., can a student articulate the assumptions behind his or her reasoning?)	Why do you react to the story in that way? What role do values and beliefs play in your perspective?	Clarity, justification, importance, consistency
5. Concept mastery (e.g., can students recognize underlying principles and concepts in an argument or text?)	How does the concept of _____ contribute to your understanding of story elements?	Depth, clarity, relevance
6. Evidence (e.g., can students present data to support a claim/issue/idea that they express in written or oral form?)	What are the reasons for your point of view? Why do you think _____ is better than _____? Provide evidence.	Relevance, adequacy, consistency
7. Inferences (e.g., can students draw accurate inferences from what they read, write, say, or hear?)	What inference do you draw from the author's ending about what happens to ___? What is your conclusion to the essay?	Relevance, adequacy, consistency
8. Implications and consequences (e.g., can students make valid implications from ideas and data provided to them?)	What plan of action could be developed based on your reading of the textbook censorship issue?	Significance, realism

Although these elements of reasoning are not directly assessed in the unit, they are applied in the teaching of all the language arts through several approaches:

▼ Each question cluster for discussion uses the key elements of reasoning as a backdrop.

▼ The research model is patterned on the reasoning process model.

▼ The argument model promoted in writing assignments stresses the elements of purpose, evidence, and conclusions.

▼ Oral presentations observed and presented by students are organized and critiqued using selected elements of reasoning.

▼ Listening activities call for students to identify speaker purpose, evidence for ideas, and conclusion.

Summary

The overall goals of the units, then, are listed below. Within the units, alignment charts are presented in the introduction and at the beginning of each lesson to demonstrate the connections of the goals to individual lessons.

Content Goals:

Goal 1: To develop analytical and interpretive skills in literature.

Goal 2: To develop persuasive writing skills.

Goal 3: To develop linguistic competency.

Goal 4: To develop listening/oral communication skills.

Process Goal:

Goal 5: To develop reasoning skills.

Concept Goal:

Goal 6: To develop an understanding of the concept of change.

▼ B. Assessment

Assessment in the units is ongoing and comprised of multiple options. Pre- and post-tests assess student growth in literature and persuasive writing. These serve multiple purposes. Performance on the pre-assessments establishes a baseline against which performance on the post-assessment may be compared. In addition, teachers may use information obtained from the pre-assessments as an aid to instructional planning as strengths and weaknesses of individual students become apparent.

The development of performance assessments for the units was based on a careful study of several sources, including the National Assessment of Educational Progress 1990 Portfolio Study (National Center for Educational Statistics, 1992) and the Reading Framework (National Assessment Governing Board, 1992). The assessment approaches developed for the series of units were intended to span the four language arts strands and the designated grade levels at 2–11. The literature selections and writing prompts are tailored to each unit of study. Authentic means of performance assessment were developed and incorporated for each strand, with the activities serving both as assessments and learning experiences.

The purposes of the performance-based assessment approach used in the units are as follows:

▼ *To assess learner outcomes of significance in the classroom*
By comparing pre-post results in a unit of study, teachers can understand how much high-ability students have grown in the particular dimension of the curriculum under study. Such data also provide a deeper insight into areas of growth still needed.

▼ *To derive important data for planning appropriate instruction (pre-assessment function)*
Pre-assessment allows teachers to see where students are functioning in respect to a particular type of task demand. For example, who can find ideas in unfamiliar text and who cannot? These data should be used to target specific teaching toward students needing it in some aspect of the language arts, based on pre-assessment results.

▼ *To determine needed emphases in the instructional process*
The performance assessments provide data for teachers to decide what aspects of instruction need more attention. For example, if students can't elaborate appropriately, a lesson on "how to elaborate in written form" might be developed.

Teachers are encouraged to use the assessments in a dynamic way to enhance overall instruction. The assessments should therefore be treated as a part of the instructional package and should be discussed and taught to immediately after students have completed them.

Literature

Pre-assessment is based on the first literature selection of each unit; post-assessment is based on the last literature selection for each unit. Each piece of literature was carefully selected to be tailored to the unit's focus and the developmental level of the students. Regardless of the selection, each student is asked to respond to specific aspects of the reading.

The questions are intended to probe the student's ability to derive meaning from a piece of literature. The first question looks at a global notion of meaning (main idea), while the second focuses on a specific sentence in which some inference and interpretation are required. The third item not only explores the student's ability to make inferences but also reaches into the concept dimension of learner outcomes to evaluate a student's identification and interpretation of the concept of change in a piece of literature. The fourth item concentrates the student's attention on synthesis of important elements of the text into an appropriate title.

Writing

A prompt for a persuasive essay is provided with the first and last literature pieces for each unit. Students are asked to respond to an issue in a paragraph structured as follows:

1. Statement of a point of view regarding whether the selection should be required reading for the student's grade level.
2. List of three reasons to support the given point of view, with elaboration.
3. Conclusion to the argument.

In scoring the writing assessment, emphasis is placed on evaluating the quality of the student's arguments rather than on mechanics. We also encourage teachers to teach the writing rubric to students so that they can effectively use it for peer and self assessments. The use of the writing assessment model then involves multiple steps:

1. Administer pre-assessment.
2. Discuss pre-assessment piece.
3. Teach the Hamburger Model as a device to encourage student internalization of persuasive essay development.
4. Provide multiple exemplary pieces of persuasive writing for student analysis.
5. Provide students practice in developing "hamburger" paragraphs and multi-paragraph essays. Several of these should be in-class and timed (10–15 minute limit for a paragraph).
6. Teach the persuasive writing rubric to students, giving them a practice essay to score and discuss. Use student exemplars provided in the units to discuss strong, mediocre and weak responses to a particular prompt.
7. Engage students in peer and self assessment of persuasive writing on an ongoing basis.
8. Administer post-assessment for persuasive writing. Discuss prompt with students.

Additional work in other forms of writing may be found throughout the units. Approaches to assessing these writing tasks are included with the relevant lessons. They include self, peer, and teacher assessment forms that allow for multiple perspectives to coalesce using the same criteria for student performance.

Portfolio assessment techniques are encouraged for assignments in which the full writing process is implemented by the teacher. Thus, the portfolio might contain a student's prewriting sample, first draft, second draft, edited draft, and final proofed copy.

Other Assessment Tools

Teachers may find specific assessment tools with individual lessons. These include protocols for evaluating oral presentations, the unit research project, and a final written assessment on how well students understand the concept of change. These assessments may be useful in ascertaining student growth in other relevant dimensions of the language arts framework.

Teachers are encouraged to use the following to reinforce and augment the formal assessments employed in the units:

A. **Response Journal:** Each student may use a spiral notebook as a response journal. As part of a reaction to each literature selection, the student writes a response to a question that is posed about that piece of literature. The teacher is encouraged to read the journal and write comments back to the student.

B. **Writing Portfolio:** Each student may maintain a manila folder as a writing portfolio. In it, he/she chronologically arranges all formal writing assignments. At the conclusion of each writing assignment, students may be asked to prepare writing self-assessments in which they reflect upon themselves as writers.

C. **Student-Teacher Conferences:** Opportunities should be provided for each student to meet periodically with the teacher to discuss current work and plans for further development.

Although assessment is not always specified for lesson activities, it is assumed that the teacher of the units will employ the instruments provided in the lessons in assessing on-going activities and products. Pre- and post-assessment instruments also appear in the lessons in which they are to be administered and then used for instructional purposes.

▼ REFERENCES

National Assessment Governing Board. (1992). *Reading framework for the 1992 National Assessment of Educational Progress.* Washington, DC: U.S. Government Printing Office.

National Center for Education Statistics. (1992). *National assessment of educational progress's 1990 portfolio study.* Washington, DC: U.S. Department of Education.

Novak, J. D., & Gowin, D. B. (1984). *Learning how to learn.* New York: Cambridge University Press.

Paul, R. (1992). *Critical thinking: What every person needs to survive in a rapidly changing world.* Sonoma, CA: The Foundation for Critical Thinking.

APPENDIX

THE CONCEPT OF CHANGE

▼ The Concept of Change: Interdisciplinary Inquiry and Meaning

by Linda Neal Boyce

What Is Change?

Because change is a complex concept that inspires fear as well as hope, the idea of change has engaged thinkers throughout the ages and across disciplines. Change is therefore best studied as an interdisciplinary concept for several reasons. First, an understanding of change in one discipline informs the study of change in another discipline and results in important connections. Secondly, an interdisciplinary study of change provides insights into the structure of each discipline. Equally important, the increasing rate of global change resulting in social, political, and environmental upheaval, an information explosion, and a technological revolution creates an urgent need to understand the dynamics of change.

To provide a basis for understanding change as a concept, this paper explores change in several disciplines. While exploring the concepts, it identifies resources for teachers and for students that focus on change. Finally, the paper examines the way the concept of change was applied in the National Language Arts Project for High Ability Learners.

Religion and Philosophy

The *Encyclopedia of Philosophy* (Capek, 1967) and *Encyclopedia of Religion and Ethics* (Hyslop, 1910) provide overviews of change from the perspectives of religion and philosophy. Both sources agree that change is one of the most basic and pervasive features of our experience. Hyslop goes so far as to say that change is difficult to define and that it is easier to discuss the types of change. He identifies four types of change: (1) qualitative change, a change in the qualities or properties of a subject such as chemical reaction; (2) quantitative change which includes expansion, contraction, detrition, and accretion; (3) local change, or a change in the subject's position in space; and (4) formal change, a change of shape. He adds that all changes involve time which is an essential condition of change.

Historically, philosophers and theologians have not always acknowledged the existence of change (Capek, 1967; Hyslop, 1910). Ideas of God, Being, and One that are based on eternal order and perfection of nature regard time and change as illusions of finite experience. Hyslop points out that acknowledging change is crucial to inquiry; that change represents the dynamic as the source of all investigations into causes. He states, "Curiosity regarding causal agency begins with the discovery of change and terminates in explanation" (p. 357). Capek's and Hyslop's essays offer an important backdrop to our understanding of the current controversies, the intense emotion, and the values that surround the concept of change.

Social Studies

In his outline of "Social Studies within a Global Education," Kniep (1989/1991) identifies change as one of the conceptual themes for social studies and asserts, "The process of movement from one state of being to another is a universal aspect of the planet and is an inevitable part of life and living" (p. 121). He lists adaptation, cause and effect, development, evolution, growth, revolution, and time as related concepts. Kniep's comprehensive scope and sequence for social studies includes: (1) essential elements (systems, human values, persistent issues and problems, and global history); (2) conceptual themes (interdependence, change,

29

culture, scarcity, and conflict); (3) phenomenological themes (people, places, and events); and (4) persistent problem themes (peace and security, national/international development, environmental problems, and human rights). Change is both a concept to understand and an agent to consider in all social studies ideas and themes.

In discussing social change, Daniel Chirot (1985) views social change as pervasive. He states that most societies, however, delude themselves into believing that stability prevails and that unchanging norms can be a reality.

Chirot identifies demographic change, technological change, and political change as the most important causes of general social change. In his discussion of how and why critical changes have occurred, Chirot considers three transformations in social structure among the most important:

▼ The technological revolution produced by the adoption of sedentary agriculture

▼ The organizational revolution that accompanied the rise of states

▼ The current "modernization" that encompasses major changes in thought, technology, and politics (p. 761).

He points out that studying current major changes such as the increasing power of the state and the proletarianization of labor helps us understand smaller changes such as those in family structure, local political organizations, types of protest, and work habits. Because change impacts on our lives in large and small ways, we must understand and confront it.

Vogt's (1968) analysis of cultural change echoes Chirot's discussion of social change: "It can now be demonstrated from our accumulated archeological and historical data that a culture is never static, but rather that one of its most fundamental properties is change" (p. 556). Vogt cites three factors that influence change in a given culture:

▼ Any change in the ecological niche as a result of natural environmental changes or the migration of a society as when the Anasazi Indians left Mesa Verde to find new homes and lost their cultural identity in the process

▼ Any contact between two societies with different cultural patterns as when Hispanic and Native American cultures converged in New Mexico

▼ Any evolutionary change occurring within a society such as when a food-gathering society domesticates its plants and animals or incorporates technology to effect lifestyle changes.

In his discussion of cultural adaptation, Carneiro (1968) distinguishes between cultural adaptation (the adjustment of a society to its external and internal conditions) and cultural evolution (change by which a society grows complex and better integrated). Adaptation may include simplification and loss resulting from a deteriorating environment. Thus, adaptation may signal negative as well as positive changes for a cultural group.

History—the social sciences discipline that chronicles change—provides insight into specific changes from a range of perspectives. For instance, resources such as *The Timetables of History* (Grun, 1991) and the *Smithsonian Timelines of the Ancient World* (Scarre, 1993) record changes by significant annual events in the areas of history and politics; literature and theater; religion, philosophy, and learning; the visual arts; music; science and technology; and daily life. These tools allow readers to see at a glance the simultaneous events and significant people involved in changes occurring throughout the world or in a specific area.

Various scholars chronicle ideas about change on an interdisciplinary canvas. Boorstin (1983) focuses on man's need to know and the courage of those who challenged dogma at various times in history. He provides an in-depth look at the causes of change, considering such questions as why the Chinese did not "discover" Europe and America and why the Egyptians and not the Greeks invented the calendar. Tamplin (1991) demonstrates the interrelationship of personal, cultural, and societal change with discussions and illustrations of literature, visual arts, architecture, music, and the performing arts. Petroski (1992) chronicles change and investigates its origins through technology. He argues that shortcomings are the driving force for change and sees inventors as critics who have a compelling urge to tinker with things and to improve them.

Science

Echoing the call for curriculum reform that centers on an in-depth study of broad concepts, Rutherford and Ahlgren (1979) in *Science for All Americans* state:

> Some important themes pervade science, mathematics, and technology and appear over and over again, whether we are looking at an ancient civilization, the human body, or a comet. They are ideas that transcend disciplinary boundaries and prove fruitful in explanation, in theory, in observation, and in design.

Rutherford and Ahlgren proceed to recommend six themes: systems, models, constancy, patterns of change, evolution, and scale. Of the six themes, three of them—constancy, patterns of change, and evolution—focus on change or its inverse. In discussing patterns of change, Rutherford and Ahlgren identify three general categories, all of which have applicability in other disciplines: (1) changes that are steady trends, (2) changes that occur in cycles, and (3) changes that are irregular.

Sher (1993) identifies and discusses four general patterns of change: (1) steady changes: those that occur at a characteristic rate; (2) cyclic changes: those changes that repeat in cycles; (3) random changes: those changes that occur irregularly, unpredictably, and in a way that is mathematically random; and (4) chaotic change: change that appears random and irregular on the surface, but is in fact or principle predictable. She considers the understanding of chaotic change as one of the most exciting developments in recent science.

As in the other disciplines, change in science can be studied as a concept and as a specific application or type of change. For example, our view of the earth over the last 40 years has changed from a static globe model to a dynamic plate tectonics model, affecting our understanding of earthquakes, volcanoes, and other seismic events (NASA, 1988; 1990).

Language—Creative and Changing

S. I. and Alan Hayakawa in *Language in Thought and Action* (1990) state categorically, "Language . . . makes progress possible" (p. 7). They argue that reading and writing make it possible to pool experience and that "cultural and intellectual cooperation is, or should be, the great principle of human life" (p. 8). They then examine the relationships among language, thought, and behavior and how language changes thinking and behavior. For instance, they discuss how judgments stop thought therefore leading to unfounded and dangerous generalizations. They explore the changing meanings of words and point out "no word ever has exactly the same meaning twice" (p. 39). For the Hayakawas, dictionaries are not authoritative statements about words but rather historical records of the meanings of words. Finally, the Hayakawas discuss the paralyzing effects of fear of change and the anger that accompanies it. They propose that the debate around issues facing society should center on specific questions such as "What will be the results?" "Who would benefit, and by how much?" and "Who would be harmed, and to what degree?" rather than questions of "right" or "wrong." They contend that this way of thinking reflects a scientific attitude and harnesses language to accurately "map" social and individual problems, thereby enabling change.

While *Language in Thought and Action* is an eloquent manifesto about the possibilities of language, the anthology *Language Awareness* (Eschholz, Rosa, & Clark, 1982) provides a resource on specific topics. The essays cover the history of language; language in politics and propaganda; the language of advertising; media and language; jargon; names; prejudice and language; taboos and euphemisms; language play; and the responsible use of language. Each essay examines either changes in language or how language changes thinking and action. For example, in her outline of the devices of propaganda that include name calling, generalities, "plain folks" appeal, stroking, personal attacks, guilt or glory by association, bandwagon appeals, faulty cause and effect, false analogy, and testimonials, Cross (1982) examines the manipulative power of language.

The powers of language range from strident manipulation to the quiet heightening of awareness. Response to language involves a change—a change of perspective, a new understanding, an insight in the search for meaning. Coles (1989) speaks of the power of literature to give direction to life and to awaken moral sensibilities. He states, "Novels and stories are renderings of life; they cannot only keep us company, but admonish us, point us in new directions, or give us the courage to stay a given course" (p. 159).

While Coles discusses the impact of literature on private lives, Downs (1978) discusses revolutionary books throughout history in his *Books That Changed the World*. Examining such books as *The Bible*, Machiavelli's *The Prince*, Beecher's *Uncle Tom's Cabin*, Darwin's *Origin of Species*, and Freud's *The Interpretation of Dreams*, Downs attempts to discover and to analyze two categories of writings: works that were direct, immediate instruments in determining the course of events, and works that molded minds over centuries. He concludes that, "Omitting the scientists in the group, for whom these comments are less pertinent, the books [which changed the world] printed since 1500 were written by nonconformists, radicals, fanatics, revolutionists, and agitators" (p. 25).

The reading process which enables readers to search for information and meaning is an active, recursive process that includes choosing a book, reading, discussing from the reader's point of view, listening to another's point of view, reflecting and responding, and re-reading or making a new choice (Bailey, Boyce, VanTassel-Baska, 1990). Effective reading includes revising an interpretation or changing ideas, a step which is mirrored in the writing process and in speaking and listening. Kennedy (1993) sees all of the language processes—reading, writing, speaking, listening, and thinking—as complex, interrelated activities; activities that result in a dynamic, changing discourse.

Censorship reflects the public's acknowledgment and fear of the power of language to change thinking, behavior, and society at large. The debate over censorship and freedom of expression has raged for centuries and ranges from the use of racist and sexist language in literature to the effects of violence on television. Plato, one may remember, argued against allowing children to listen to imaginative stories and banned the poets from his ideal society. The continuing controversy regarding the burning of the American flag is one of several censorship issues widely debated in our society that illustrates the linkage of symbols, language, and freedom of expression (Bradbury and Quinn, 1991).

Telecommunications in a Changing World

Telecommunications has dramatically changed our capacity to access information. Electronic mail, known as e-mail, is a telecommunications system that links computers around the world through telephone lines and satellites. It has created significant changes in scientific and business communities such as: increased flexibility for team members working in various locations across time zones, an end to isolation of researchers around the world, and the restructuring of organizations by eliminating corporate hierarchies (Perry, 1992a). Perry also cites the role of e-mail in the Russian coup of Boris Yeltsin and the use of faxes during the Tiananmen uprising. E-mail and fax machines provided sources of information that were difficult to control and allowed dissenters to communicate with one another and with the outside world (Perry, 1992b).

Video, television, cable, compact discs, and computers and the Internet are transforming not only access to information, but the content of information as well. In a recent *U.S. News and World Report* article John Leo (March 8, 1993) discusses the new standard of television news that blends information and entertainment. He contends that images, story line, and emotional impact are replacing a commitment to evidence, ethics, and truth. In another development, compact discs and computers are combining sound tracks, animation, photography, and print information that replace standard multi-volume encyclopedias and that enable users to combine information in new ways. The Grolier Multimedia Encyclopedia (1994) on CD-ROM for example, supplements its text with features such as animated multimedia maps that show the growth and development of American railroads, the women's suffrage movement, and other topics. This changing information technology demands new standards for the evaluation of information and new consideration of how technology can limit or expand thinking.

The Concept of Change and Language Arts Unit Development

For the purposes of teaching the concept of change for the National Javits Language Arts Project for High Ability Learners, five generalizations about change were drawn from the literature of various disciplines. Table I illustrates those generalizations and their accompanying outcomes. Examples of how the generalizations were addressed in the units through language study, language processes, and literature follow Table I.

▼ Table I
Generalizations and Outcomes about Change

Generalizations	Outcomes
1. Change is pervasive.	Understand that change permeates our lives and our universe.
2. Change is linked to time.	Illustrate the variability of change based on time.
3. Change may be perceived as systematic or random.	Categorize types of change, given several examples. Demonstrate the change process at work in a piece of literature.
4. Change may represent growth and development or regression and decay.	Interpret change in selected works as progressive or regressive.
5. Change may occur according to natural order or be imposed by individuals or groups.	Analyze social and individual change in a given piece of literature.

Language Study

Throughout the units, word study and vocabulary served as a primary source for studying change. Students constructed vocabulary webs that mapped words by (1) the definition; (2) a sentence that used the word from the literature being studied; (3) an example of the word; and (4) an analysis of the word that identified stems (roots, prefixes, and suffixes), word families, and word history. To build on the verbal talent of high-ability learners, resources such as *Sumer Is Icumen In: Our Ever-Changing Language* by Greenfeld (1978) and *Oxford Guide to Word Games* by Augarde (1984) were included in the units to encourage students to explore language changes and to play with the possibilities of inventing it themselves.

Each unit included a grammar packet developed by Michael Thompson and based on his work, *The Magic Lens: A Spiral Tour through the Human Ideas of Grammar* (1991). Thompson's packets were designed to help students learn why some ideas are clear and others are confusing; to understand the power of grammar to reveal deep thinking and deep meaning. Implicit in this study was the idea that changing the grammar of a sentence or paragraph meant changing its meaning. Literature selections upon which the units were built and the students' own writing provided the context for studying grammar.

Language Processes

The processes of reading, writing, listening, and speaking were studied as change processes. Literature discussions were based on the premise that each person's interpretation and understanding of meaning would be different from another person's interpretation. Through listening to one another, students were encouraged to seek new meaning and to examine how their interpretations changed during the discussion. In like manner, students studied the writing process as a way to explore ideas and to generate their own thinking and learning. The revision stage of writing emphasized seeking feedback and listening to responses from teachers and peers. Considering another's perspective often led to changes in the understanding of one's own work and to subsequent changes in the structure and clarity of the writing.

Oral communications in these units centered on persuasive speaking and critical listening. Students studied how to change their audience's opinion and actions through argument formulation and strategies of persuasion. As students listened to persuasive speeches, they analyzed the arguments and evaluated their effectiveness. Resources for the speaking and listening components included videotapes of master persuaders such as Franklin D. Roosevelt, Martin Luther King, Jr., and Adolf Hitler that provided students with opportunities to consider the role of persuasion in social and historical contexts. Other resources such as *The American Reader: Words That Moved a Nation* (Ravitch, 1990) documented the persuasive role of oral communications such as orations, Congressional hearings, and songs in the process of change.

Literature

Each of the units was developed around literature selections with vocabulary and language study emerging from the selections. The development of the concept of change also emerged from the literature discussions and activities. Typically each literary piece was examined for evidence of character changes, both physical and psychological, as well as social, political, and economic changes. For instance, in "The Power of Light" by I. B. Singer (1962), students discussed the issue of whether characters change themselves or are changed by events outside of their control.

In addition to the literature selections which were discussed with the total group, additional resources embedded in each unit illustrated the generalizations about change and addressed the social, cultural and environmental implications of change. For instance, *Commodore Perry in the Land of the Shogun* (Blumberg, 1985) documents the dramatic social and cultural changes created by Perry's visits to Japan in 1853 and 1854. Illustrated with reproductions of primary sources, the account presents misconceptions, hostilities, and humorous episodes encountered from multiple points of view. Change is palpable while reading the book. A very different book, *Letting Swift River Go* by Yolen (1992) tells of the drowning of a Swift River town for the building of the Quabbin Reservoir, a water supply for Boston and now a wilderness area. The open-ended story alludes to necessary tradeoffs and provides opportunities to discuss changes linked to time as well as the positive and negative aspects of change.

Conclusion

The idea of change crosses all disciplines and offers learners an opportunity to construct a concept that will inform their lives in meaningful ways. Because of the accelerating rate of change in our world, students need to understand the concept and to acquire effective tools for meeting its challenges. Language with its powers of inquiry, persuasion, and critique provides a powerful tool for meeting the challenges of change.

Literature, in particular, offers students and teachers a rich content arena for analyzing change and for considering the issues that surround it. Literature captures the voices, the emotions, and the concerns of thinkers through the ages and across cultures. It demonstrates types of change, responses to change, the causes and agents of change, as well as the effects of change. In a time of dizzying change, literature also offers continuity and a welcomed opportunity for reflection.

▼ REFERENCES

Augarde, T. (1984). *The Oxford guide to word games.* Oxford: Oxford University Press.

Bailey, J. M., Boyce, L. N., & VanTassel-Baska, J. (1990). The writing, reading, and counseling connection: A framework for serving the gifted. In J. VanTassel-Baska (Ed.), *A practical guide to counseling the gifted in a school setting* (2nd ed.) (pp. 72–89). Reston, VA: The Council for Exceptional Children.

Blumberg, R. (1985). *Commodore Perry in the land of the shogun.* New York: Lothrop.

Boorstin, D. J. (1983). *The Discoverers: A history of man's search to know his world and himself.* New York: Random.

Bradbury, N. M., & Quinn, A. (1991). *Audiences and intentions: A book of arguments.* New York: Macmillan.

Capek, M. (1967). Change. In P. Edwards (Ed.), *The encyclopedia of philosophy* (Vol. 1, pp. 75–79). New York: Macmillan.

Carneiro, R. L. (1968). Cultural adaptation. In D. L. Sills (Ed.), *International encyclopedia of the social sciences* (Vol. 3, pp. 551–554). New York: Macmillan & The Free Press.

Chirot, D. (1985). Social change. In A. Kuper & J. Kuper (Eds.), *The social science encyclopedia* (pp. 760–763). Boston: Routledge & Kegan Paul.

Coles, R. (1989). *The call of stories: Teaching and the moral imagination.* Boston: Houghton Mifflin.

Cross, D. W. (1982). Propaganda: How not to be bamboozled. In P. Eschholz, A. Rosa, & V. Clark (Eds.), *Language awareness* (pp. 70–81). New York: St. Martin's.

Downs, R. B. (1978). *Books that changed the world* (2nd ed). Chicago, IL: American Library Association.

Eschholz, P., Rosa, A., & Clark, V. (1982). *Language awareness* (3rd ed.). New York: St. Martin's.

Greenfeld, H. (1978). *Sumer is icumen in: Our ever-changing language.* New York: Crown.

Grolier multimedia encyclopedia (1994). Danbury, CT: Grolier.

Grun, B. (1991). *The timetables of history: A horizontal linkage of people and events*. New York: Simon & Schuster.

Hayakawa, S. I., & Hayakawa, A. R. (1990). *Language in thought and action* (5th ed.). Fort Worth, TX: Harcourt Brace Jovanovich.

Hyslop, J. H. (1910). Change. In J. Hastings (Ed.), *Encyclopaedia of religion and ethics* (Vol. 3, pp. 357–358). New York: Scribner's.

Kennedy, C. (1993). Teaching with writing: The state of the art. In *Language arts topics papers*. Williamsburg, VA: College of William and Mary, Center for Gifted Education.

Kniep, W. M. (1991). Appendix 3: Social studies within a global education. In W. C. Parker (Ed.), *Renewing the social studies curriculum* (pp. 119–123). Alexandria, VA: Association for Supervision and Curriculum Development. (Reprinted from *Social Education*, 1989, pp. 399–403.)

Leo, J. (1993, March 8). Spicing up the (ho-hum) truth. *U.S. News & World Report, 14*(9), 24.

National Aeronautics and Space Administration. (1988). *Earth system science: A program for global change*. Washington, DC: NASA.

National Aeronautics and Space Administration. (1990). *The earth observing system: A mission to planet earth*. Washington, DC: NASA.

Newmann, F. M., & Wehlage, G. G. (1993). Five standards of authentic instruction. *Educational Leadership, 50*(7), 8–12.

Perry, T. S. (1992a, October). E-mail at work. *IEEE Spectrum, 29*(10), 24–28.

Perry, T. S. (1992b, October). Forces for social change. *IEEE Spectrum, 29*(10), 30–32.

Petroski, H. (1992). *The evolution of useful things*. New York: Knopf.

Ravitch, D. (1990). *The American reader: Words that moved a nation*. New York: HarperCollins.

Rutherford, F. J., & Ahlgren, A. (1989). *Science for all Americans: Scientific literacy*. New York: American Association for the Advancement of Science.

Scarre, C. (Ed.). (1993). *Smithsonian timelines of the ancient world: A visual chronology from the origins of life to AD 1500*. New York: Dorling.

Seiger-Ehrenberg, S. (1991). Concept development. In A. L. Costa (Ed.), *Developing minds* (Rev. ed., Vol. 1, pp. 290–294). Alexandria, VA: Association for Supervision and Curriculum Development.

Sher, B. T. (1993). *Guide to science concepts: Developing science curriculum for high-ability learners K–8*. Williamsburg, VA: College of William and Mary, School of Education, Center for Gifted Education.

Singer, I. B. (1962). *Stories for children*. New York: Farrar, Straus, Giroux.

Tamplin, R. (Ed.). (1991). *The arts: A history of expression in the 20th century*. New York: Free Press.

Thompson, M. C. (1991). *The magic lens: A spiral tour through the human ideas of grammar*. Unionville, NY: Trillium.

Vogt, E. Z. (1968). Culture Change. In D. L. Sills (Ed.), *International encyclopedia of the social sciences*, Vol. 3 (pp. 554–558). New York: Macmillan & The Free Press.

Yolen, J. (1992). *Letting Swift River go*. Boston: Little, Brown.

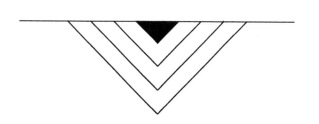

SECTION
III

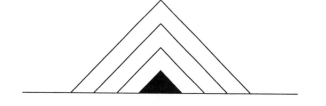

IMPLEMENTATION

▼ A. CLASSROOM GUIDELINES

The following pages provide guidelines for teachers on implementing the units effectively in classrooms. Comments from teachers who piloted the units have been used in developing these recommendations.

Target Population

The units were designed for use with high-ability students in second through eleventh grade. They have been piloted with such students in various settings and found effective with respect to learning gains. In heterogeneous settings, the units have been used with a broader range of students and found effective as well, provided that teachers have modified the reading selections.

Use of the Units in Relation to Existing Language Arts Curriculum

Each unit is intended to represent a semester's work in language arts for high-ability learners. Thus, whoever teaches a unit should assign the grade for language arts and note individual progress based on the goals of the unit. Because the units do not include specific lesson emphases on spelling, developmental reading skills, or narrative writing, it is recommended that these elements be considered for use during a second semester of language arts. Supplemental materials might include *Junior Great Books*, *Write Source 2000*, *The Magic Lens*, and *Word within the Word*. (See Language Arts Resources for Teachers in Section VI for references.)

Schedule for Unit Implementation

A unit lesson is defined as at least one two-hour session. It is preferable that the units be taught across a two-hour block that encompasses both reading and language arts time allocations. A minimum of fifty total instructional hours should be allocated for teaching each unit. Teachers are encouraged to expand this schedule based on available time and student interest. Many teachers have used a given unit for a full semester of work. Ideally, this curriculum should be taught in a setting in which the class meets on a daily basis.

Grouping

The units have been implemented in a variety of classroom grouping models, including heterogeneous classrooms, pull-out programs, and self-contained gifted classes. Based on our feedback from national pilots, we suggest that school districts employ their existing grouping approach to teach the units the first time. Based on individual district results from the first year of implementation, decisions about regrouping procedures may be explored. The comments that follow relate to implementation tips for each setting:

Inclusion or Heterogeneous Classrooms

▼ In this type of setting, it is recommended that teachers differentiate the readings for implementation. Readings provided with the units are clearly intended for advanced readers.

▼ It is also advisable to cluster group students based on reading selections for discussion of these readings.

▼ All students can benefit from learning the fundamental teaching models employed in the units.

▼ The research projects may be modified for students, based on individual level of functioning.

Pull-out Programs

▼ Students must meet at least two hours per week in order to implement a unit.

▼ Cross-grade grouping might be considered in order to implement a unit.

▼ Continuity of ideas is the challenge in implementing a unit in this program context. It is essential that homework be assigned and completed, even within a pull-out program that does not meet daily.

Self-contained Gifted Classes

▼ In this setting, the units need to be supplemented with other materials and resources. Use of *Junior Great Books* to enhance literature study is recommended. Michael Thompson's materials in vocabulary and grammar are also recommended. (See Part VI for references.)

▼ Cluster grouping is encouraged to ensure that more advanced readers are grouped together.

Use of Learning Centers

Learning centers should be set up and made available for student use throughout the course of teaching the units. They help to provide a change of pace during large time blocks of instruction as well as allowing students to explore topics of interest more fully. They are introduced in the lesson plans as they become relevant to the aspects of the unit being studied. Learning centers may be managed as the teacher sees fit, with specific times assigned to these activities or on a less structured basis. It would be helpful to have an assistant to interact with students and answer questions during learning center time. Some recording system should be established; a notebook of student records may be kept at each learning center, or students may keep records in their individual unit notebooks.

A list of sample recommended learning centers includes the following:

a. **Language Study Center**

This Learning Center is intended to provide students with additional opportunities to study language. A set of teacher-made task cards should be kept at the Center with short tasks or projects for students; they may keep a record in their notebooks of task card responses. Task cards may include several activities with different levels of difficulty, and points or scores may be assigned accordingly if the teacher chooses. Several sample task cards are listed on the next page:

Card 1: *Write the sentence below on a card. Ask at least ten people to read it out loud. Note the way they pronounce the word "February." Look up the pronunciation in a good dictionary. Write a paragraph telling about your "pronunciation survey" and its results.*

Valentine's Day comes in February.

Card 2: *Make two word banks that list words that can be used to describe the actions of a) drinking and b) eating. Then substitute an appropriate form of each into the following sentence to see how much difference each makes in the meaning.*

Alfred _____ the milk and _____ the cookies.

Card 3: *Look for some words that do not contain the letters **a, e, i, o,** or **u.** List them.*

Card 4: *Look up the word "anagram" in a dictionary.*

  a) *Write the definition.*

  b) *Analyze the meaning of the word using the Latin meanings of the parts of the word.*

  c) *Make a list of 20 pairs of words that are anagram pairs.*

Card 5: *Look up the meanings of the words "further" and "farther." Write an explanation of how each should be used. Then write each one in a sentence.*

b. **Unit Vocabulary Center**

At this Learning Center, a list of new vocabulary words encountered in the unit readings should be kept and regularly updated. Dictionaries and blank copies of the Vocabulary Web should be kept at the Center, as well as copies of student readings. Students visiting the Center may work alone or in small groups to develop Vocabulary Webs from unit words, either compiling individual notebooks of webs or a class notebook. This Center allows students to gain more practice with the Vocabulary Web, as class time will not allow all of the new words to be studied in depth.

c. **Writing/Computer Center**

At this Learning Center, students have the opportunity to practice the stages of writing and the format of the persuasive paragraph. Writing materials and a word processing program should be made available to students, along with a list of suggested writing topics. Students may compose paragraphs and longer pieces at the Writing/Computer Center, may work in pairs to critique one another's work, and may revise, edit, and publish their work. This Center may be used to work on unit assignments and/or on separate extension activities.

d. **Persuasive Speaking Center**

At this Learning Center, videos of speeches are available for students to watch and analyze according to their growing understanding of elements of persuasion. Encourage them to evaluate the speeches they watch, using the materials they are given to evaluate presentations in class. The Center should also have available a list of prompts for persuasive speeches students may develop and deliver themselves to a small group of peers or to the class.

e. **Research Center**

This Learning Center may include a regular and an electronic encyclopedia, nonfiction books, and other resources which will help students in investigating their issue. A list of guiding questions and key terms to investigate may help students in their research efforts. In addition, this Center may include nonfiction materials about the authors whose works are included in the unit as well as the people, places, and things described in the readings, so that students may pursue areas of interest.

Use of Technology

Various elements of technology are used to enhance the effectiveness of each unit.

▼ A word processing program may be used for writing, revising, and editing written work. Students should be expected to use a spell checker to assist in the editing process.

▼ The research strand requires students to locate data and evidence to support various points of view on their issue. The following information-gathering tools may be useful to students as they seek ideas and information. Teachers should ensure that students understand each information source and how to access it:
  ▼ CD-ROM library databases
  ▼ Interview or survey by electronic mail
  ▼ Specific resource materials on CD-ROM such as an encyclopedia, atlas, or other reference materials
  ▼ World Wide Web

Collaboration with Librarians

Because literature and information play key roles in the search for meaning, the units depend on rich and extensive library resources. Working with librarians is essential for both teachers and students throughout each unit. Teachers and school librarians should work together in the planning stages to tailor the literature and research demands to the interests and abilities of the students. Because many of the resources suggested in the units exceed the scope of school libraries, public and academic librarians should also be involved in the planning and implementation. Librarians can suggest resources, obtain materials on interlibrary loan, and work with students on research projects.

Students should be encouraged to become acquainted with the librarians in their community for several reasons. First, libraries are complex systems of organizing information. The systems vary from one library to another, and technological access to the systems is constantly changing. Librarians serve as expert guides to the information maze, and they are eager to assist library users. Secondly, the most important skill in using the library is knowing how to ask questions. Students should learn that working with a librarian is not a one-time inquiry or plea for assistance, but an interactive communication and discovery process. As the student asks a question and the librarian makes suggestions, the student will gain a better understanding of the topic and find new questions and ideas to explore. To maximize the use of library resources, the student should then discuss these new questions and ideas with the librarian. Learning to use the services of librarians and other information professionals is an important tool for lifelong learning.

▼ B. TEACHING MODELS

There are seven teaching models that are used consistently throughout the units to ensure emphasis on unit outcomes. It is suggested that teachers become familiar with these models and how to implement them before using the units. The models are listed below and outlined in the pages that follow.

1. The Taba Model of Concept Development
2. Literature Web Model
3. Vocabulary Web Model
4. Hamburger Model for Persuasive Writing
5. The Writing Process Model
6. Elements of Reasoning
7. Research Model

The Taba Model of Concept Development

The concept development model used in the units, based on Hilda Taba's Concept Development model (Taba, 1962), involves both inductive and deductive reasoning processes. Used as a beginning lesson in each unit, the model focuses on the creation of generalizations from a student-derived list of created concepts. The model is comprised of five steps and involves student participation at every step. Students begin with a broad concept, determine specific examples from that, create appropriate categorization systems, establish a generalization from those categories, and then apply the generalization to their readings and other situations.

This model is best employed by dividing the class into small groups of 4–5 for initial work, followed by whole class discussion after each stage of the process. The explanation below illustrates the use of the model around the concept of change, the central idea of each unit.

1. Students generate examples of the concept of change, derived from their own understanding and experiences with changes in the world. Teachers should encourage students to provide at least 25 examples.

2. Once an adequate number of examples has been elicited, students then group examples together into categories. Such a process allows students to search for interrelatedness and to organize materials. Students should explain their reasoning for given categories and seek clarification from each other as a whole class. Teachers should ensure that students have accounted for all of their examples through the categories established.

3. Students are now asked to think of non-examples of the concept of change. Teachers may begin the brainstorming process with the direction to list examples of things that *do not change*. Teachers should encourage students to think carefully about non-examples and discuss ideas within their groups. Each group should list five to six non-examples.

4. The students now determine generalizations about the concept of change, using their lists of examples and non-examples. Generalizations might include such ideas as "Change may be positive or negative" and "Change is linked to time." Generalizations should be derived from student input and may not precisely reflect the unit generalizations. Teachers should post the students' best generalizations on one side of the room and the prescribed unit generalizations on the other. Each set should be referred to throughout the unit.

5. Throughout the units, students are asked to identify specific examples of the generalizations from their own readings, or to describe how the concept of change applies to a given situation about which they have read. Students are also asked to apply the generalizations to their own writings and their own lives.

Source: Taba, H. (1962). *Curriculum development: Theory and practice.* New York: Harcourt, Brace & World.

Practice webs using the generalizations about change are structured into core lessons in each unit. A change matrix asking students to link ideas about change to the literature they read is used throughout the units. A final assessment on how well students understand the concept of change may also be found in one of the concluding lessons of each unit.

The concept of change is discussed more fully in the paper in the Appendix to Part II of this guide.

Literature Web Model

The Literature Web model encourages students to consider five aspects of a selection they are reading: key words (important, interesting, intriguing, surprising, or unknown to the reader), feelings (those of the reader), images or symbols, ideas, and structure of writing (anything you notice about how the piece is written, such as dialogue, rhyming, short sentences, or big words). The web helps students to organize their initial responses and provides them with a platform for discussing the piece in small or large groups. Whenever possible, students should be allowed to underline and to make marginal notes as they read and reread. After marking the text, they then organize their notes into the web.

Suggested questions for completing and discussing the web are described below:

a. **Key Words:** Think and look back over the story. What were some words or groups of words that you really liked or thought were really important? Why were they special words to you? What were some words that you thought were interesting or exciting?

b. **Feelings:** What feelings did you get when you read the story? What feelings do you think the characters had? What happened in the story to tell you how the characters were feeling? Why do you think you had the feelings that you did?

c. **Ideas:** What was the main idea of the story? What were some of the other ideas the author was trying to talk about? What was she saying about change?

d. **Images:** What were some of the pictures that came to your mind as you read the story? What were some things about the story that may have had more than one meaning?

e. **Structure of Writing:** What are some important characteristics of the way this piece is put together? How does the rhyming pattern (or dialogue, short sentences, etc.) contribute to the piece? How is the structure important for the meaning of the piece?

After students have completed their webs individually, they should compare their webs in small groups. This initial discussion will enable them to consider the ideas of others and to understand that individuals interpret literature differently. These small groups may compile a composite web that includes the ideas of all members.

Following the small group work, teachers have several options for using the webs. For instance, they may ask each group to report to the class; they may ask groups to post their composite webs; or they may develop a new web with the class based on the small group work. However, each web serves to prepare students to consider various issues the teacher will raise in whole group discussion. It is important that teachers hold a whole group discussion as the final aspect of implementing the model as a teaching-learning device. Teachers are encouraged to post the poem or story under consideration on an overhead or wherever it can be seen as the discussion is held. The teacher should record ideas, underline words listed, and call attention to student responses visually.

▼ Literature Web Model

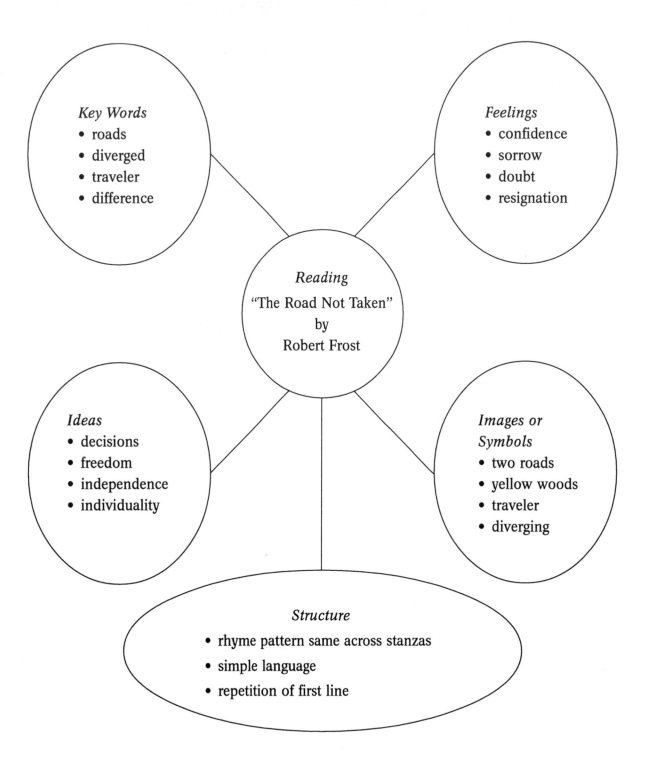

Key Words
- roads
- diverged
- traveler
- difference

Feelings
- confidence
- sorrow
- doubt
- resignation

Reading
"The Road Not Taken"
by
Robert Frost

Ideas
- decisions
- freedom
- independence
- individuality

Images or Symbols
- two roads
- yellow woods
- traveler
- diverging

Structure
- rhyme pattern same across stanzas
- simple language
- repetition of first line

▼ Vocabulary Web Model

The purpose of the Vocabulary Web model is to enable students to gain an in-depth understanding of interesting words. Rather than promoting superficial vocabulary development, the web approach allows for deep student processing of challenging and interesting words.

An example of a vocabulary web activity is given below. The teacher should introduce the activity by exploring the web with the whole class. General steps are listed below, with the word *diverge* as an example:

1. Introduce a **Vocabulary Web**. Put students in groups of no more than four, with a dictionary available as a resource in each group. Distribute copies of a blank Vocabulary Web and ask students to write the word *diverge* in the center. Ask for an explanation of what the word means within the context of a given piece of literature. Have students find the word in the story and write the sentence in which it is found in the "Sentence" cell of the Vocabulary Web.

2. Ask students to look in their dictionaries to find the definition of the word. Display an enlarged copy of the definition on the board or overhead. Have students write the definition relevant to the story into the "Definition" cell of the Vocabulary Web.

3. In their groups, have students develop their own sentences using the word. Ask them to write the sentence in the "Example" cell.

4. Discuss the meanings of the words *synonym* and *antonym*. Have students check the dictionary and think about possible synonyms and antonyms for the word and fill them into the appropriate cells. [Note: Not all cells must be filled for all words; there may not be synonyms and antonyms for all of the words studied.]

5. Ask students what is meant by the phrase "part of speech." Have them locate the part of the dictionary definition that identifies a word's part of speech. Students should then write the part of speech for the word *diverge* into their group webs.

6. Encourage students to think about the *stems* of the word, or the smaller words and pieces of words from which the larger word is made. These include prefixes, suffixes, and roots. Encourage students to check the dictionary for possible stems. Write any identified stems into the appropriate cell of the Vocabulary Web.

7. Have students locate the origin of the word (Latin, French, Greek, etc.) in the definition and write it in the "Origin" cell of the Vocabulary Web.

8. Ask students to think of other words in the same family as the word *diverge*, or other words which use one or more of the same stems. Encourage them to use their ideas from the stems cell to give them ideas.

9. Discuss the Vocabulary Webs developed by the student groups.

Note: Students may also add any number of extensions to the main circles if they identify additional information about the word.

Once students become familiar with this activity, they should use a streamlined version to accommodate new words they meet in their independent reading. A vocabulary section should be kept in a separate place in students' notebooks for this purpose. They need list only the word, definition, and sentence in which the word was encountered, plus any additional information they find particularly interesting, and they may then develop webs for a few selected words. *The American Heritage Dictionary of the English Language* (Third Edition) is recommended for this purpose.

▼ Vocabulary Web Model

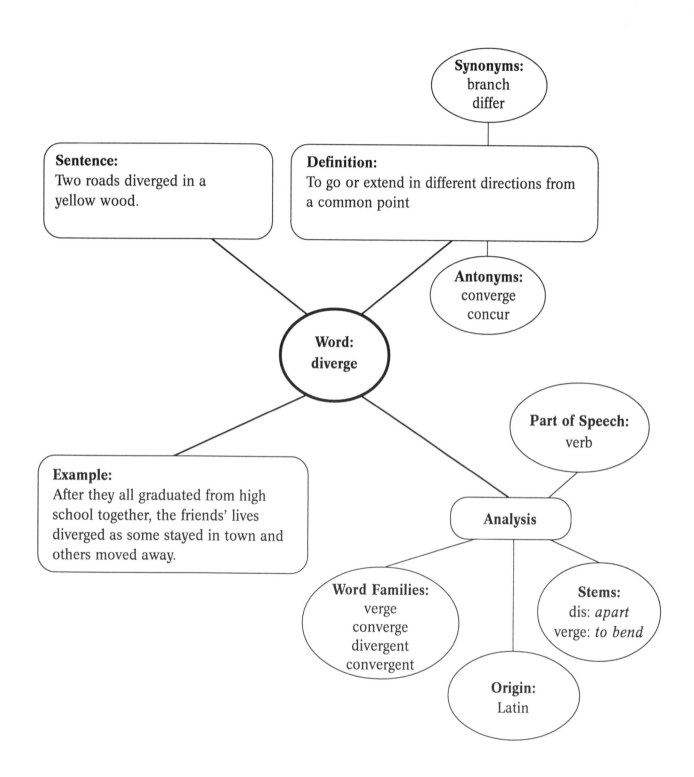

Synonyms:
branch
differ

Sentence:
Two roads diverged in a
yellow wood.

Definition:
To go or extend in different directions from
a common point

Antonyms:
converge
concur

Word:
diverge

Part of Speech:
verb

Example:
After they all graduated from high
school together, the friends' lives
diverged as some stayed in town and
others moved away.

Analysis

Word Families:
verge
converge
divergent
convergent

Stems:
dis: *apart*
verge: *to bend*

Origin:
Latin

▼ The Hamburger Model for Persuasive Writing

The purpose of the Hamburger Model is to provide students with a useful metaphor to aid them in developing a persuasive paragraph or essay. The model should be introduced by the teacher, showing students that the top bun and the bottom bun represent the introduction and conclusion of any persuasive writing piece. The teacher should note that the reasons given in support of the thesis statement are like the meat or vegetables in a hamburger, providing the major substance of the sandwich. Elaboration represents the condiments in a sandwich, the ketchup, mustard, and onions that hold a sandwich together, just as examples and illustrations hold a persuasive writing piece together.

Teachers should show students examples of hamburger paragraphs and essays and have students find the top bun, bottom bun, hamburger, and condiments. Discuss how "good" each sandwich is.

Teachers may now ask students to construct their own "hamburger" paragraphs. After students have constructed their own paragraphs, teachers may use peer and self assessments to have students judge their own and one another's writing. This process should be repeated throughout the teaching of each unit.

The Dagwood (or Club) version of the model is introduced in several of the units for older students. It is an elaborated version of the Hamburger paragraph or essay.

▼ THE HAMBURGER MODEL FOR PERSUASIVE WRITING

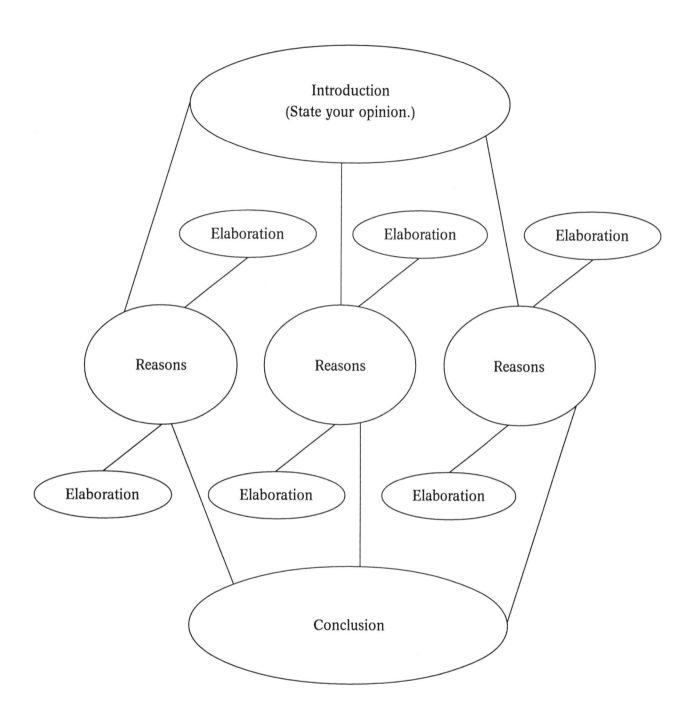

▼ THE DAGWOOD (OR CLUB) ESSAY MODEL FOR PERSUASIVE WRITING

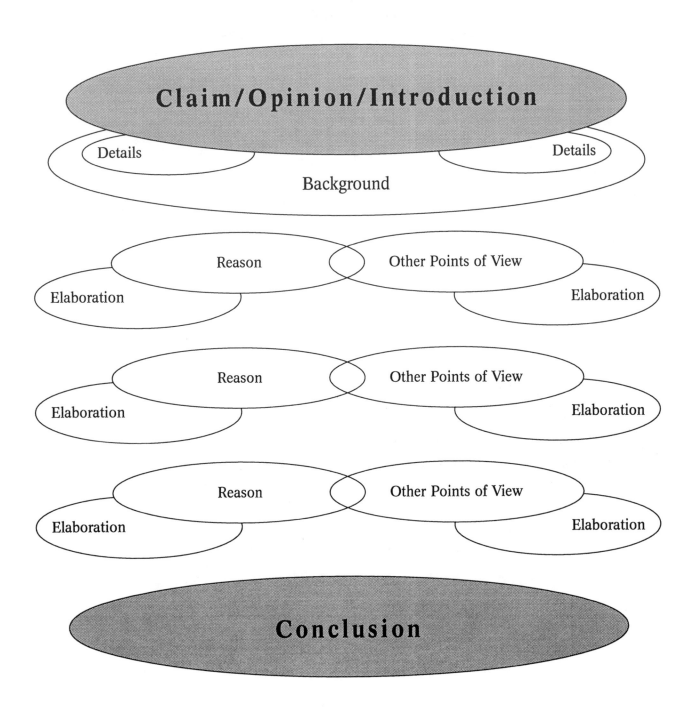

▼ THE WRITING PROCESS MODEL

The writing process shows the stages that writers use to develop a written composition. The stages are not separate parts that writers go through from one to five; rather, writers move back and forth among the stages and use them to construct, clarify, and polish their writing. The writing process model is used throughout the unit to encourage students to engage in actively improving their own writing.

1. *Prewriting:* List your ideas and begin to organize them. You may want to use a graphic organizer such as a web or a Venn diagram. Graphic organizers help you to "see" what you will write about. As you write, you can add to your diagram or change it.

2. *Drafting:* Write a rough draft, getting your ideas onto paper and not worrying about mechanics such as spelling, grammar, or punctuation. Some writers call this stage "composing." Sometimes the first draft is a "messing around" stage in which your drafting or composing helps you to "hear" what you want to say.

3. *Revising:* Conferencing is an essential step in the revising stage. Ask people (friends, family, teachers) to read and listen to your work and to tell you what they like, what they don't understand, and what they'd like to know more about. This is the place to make major changes in your "composition" or draft. Sometimes you may want to go back to the prewriting stage and redo your organizer so that your paper has a new structure.

4. *Editing:* After you have revised your paper, look for the small changes that will make a big difference. Check your choice of words and identify mechanical errors. After you make the changes and corrections, proofread your work one final time. You may want to ask a friend or an adult for help.

5. *Sharing or Publishing:* There are numerous ways to share and to publish your work. You can bind it into a book, recopy it in your best handwriting and post it on a bulletin board, read it aloud to your class or family, or make it into a gift for someone special.

▼ Elements of Reasoning

The reasoning strand used throughout the units focuses on eight elements identified by Richard Paul (1992). It is embedded in all lessons of the units through questions, writing assignments, and research work. These elements of thought are the basic building blocks of productive thinking. Working together, they provide a general logic to reasoning. In literature interpretation and listening, they help one make sense of the reasoning of the author or speaker. In writing and speaking, they enable authors or speakers to strengthen their arguments.

Students are often asked to distinguish between facts and opinions. However, between pure opinion and hard facts lie reasoned judgments in which beliefs are supported by reasons. Instruction in this area needs to be included in all forms of communication in the language arts.

The eight elements of reasoning are introduced to students in a specific unit lesson. Teachers may use the elements to assist in crafting questions for class discussion of literature or questions for probing student thinking. Examples of such questions are given on the Wheel of Reasoning that follows the descriptions below.

The eight elements of reasoning are as follows:

1. **Purpose, Goal, or End View**

   We reason to achieve some objective, to satisfy a desire, to fulfill some need. For example, if the car does not start in the morning, the purpose of my reasoning is to figure out a way to get to work. One source of problems in reasoning is traceable to "defects" at the level of purpose or goal. If our goal itself is unrealistic, contradictory to other goals we have, confused or muddled in some way, then the reasoning we use to achieve it is problematic. If we are clear on the purpose for our writing and speaking, it will help focus the message in a coherent direction. The purpose in our reasoning might be to persuade others. When we read and listen, we should be able to determine the author's or speaker's purpose.

2. **Question at Issue (or Problem to Be Solved)**

   When we attempt to reason something out, there is at least one question at issue or problem to be solved (if not, there is no reasoning required). If we are not clear about what the question or problem is, it is unlikely that we will find a reasonable answer, or one that will serve our purpose. As part of the reasoning process, we should be able to formulate the question to be answered or the issue to be addressed. For example, why won't the car start? or should libraries censor materials that contain objectionable language?

3. **Points of View or Frame of Reference**

   As we take on an issue, we are influenced by our own point of view. For example, parents of young children and librarians might have different points of view on censorship issues. The price of a shirt may seem low to one person while it seems high to another because of a different frame of reference. Any defect in our point of view or frame of reference is a possible source of problems in our reasoning. Our point of view may be too narrow, may not be precise enough, may be unfairly biased, and so forth. By considering multiple points of view, we may sharpen or broaden our thinking. In writing and speaking, we may strengthen our arguments by acknowledging other points of view. In listening and reading, we need to identify the perspective of the speaker or author and understand how it affects the message delivered.

4. **Experiences, Data, Evidence**

When we reason, we must be able to support our point of view with reasons or evidence. Evidence is important in order to distinguish opinions from reasons or to create a reasoned judgment. Evidence and data should support the author's or speaker's point of view and can strengthen an argument. An example is data from surveys or published studies. In reading and listening, we can evaluate the strength of an argument or the validity of a statement by examining the supporting data or evidence. Experiences can also contribute to the data of our reasoning. For example, previous experiences in trying to get a car to start may contribute to the reasoning process that is necessary to resolve the problem.

5. **Concepts and Ideas**

Reasoning requires the understanding and use of concepts and ideas (including definitional terms, principles, rules, or theories). When we read and listen, we can ask ourselves, "What are the key ideas presented?" When we write and speak, we can examine and organize our thoughts around the substance of concepts and ideas. Some examples of concepts are freedom, friendship, and responsibility.

6. **Assumptions**

We need to take some things for granted when we reason. We need to be aware of the assumptions we have made and the assumptions of others. If we make faulty assumptions, this can lead to defects in reasoning. As a writer or speaker we make assumptions about our audience and our message. For example, we might assume that others will share our point of view; or we might assume that the audience is familiar with the First Amendment when we refer to "First Amendment rights." As a reader or listener we should be able to identify the assumptions of the writer or speaker.

7. **Inferences**

Reasoning proceeds by steps called inferences. An inference is a small step of the mind, in which a person concludes that something is so because of something else being so or seeming to be so. The tentative conclusions (inferences) we make depend on what we assume as we attempt to make sense of what is going on around us. For example, we see dark clouds and infer that it is going to rain; or we know the movie starts at 7:00; it is now 6:45; it takes 30 minutes to get to the theater; so we cannot get there on time. Many of our inferences are justified and reasonable, but many are not. We need to distinguish between the raw data of our experiences and our interpretations of those experiences (inferences). Also, the inferences we make are heavily influenced by our point of view and our assumptions.

8. Implications and Consequences

When we reason in a certain direction, we need to look at the consequences of that direction. When we argue and support a certain point of view, solid reasoning requires that we consider what the implications are of following that path; what are the consequences of taking the course that we support? When we read or listen to an argument, we need to ask ourselves what follows from that way of thinking. We can also consider consequences of actions that characters in stories take. For example, if I don't do my homework, I will have to stay after school to do it; if I water the lawn, it will not wither in the summer heat.

Adapted from Paul, R. (1992). *Critical thinking: What every person needs to survive in a rapidly changing world*. Sonoma, CA: Foundation for Critical Thinking.

▼ WHEEL OF REASONING

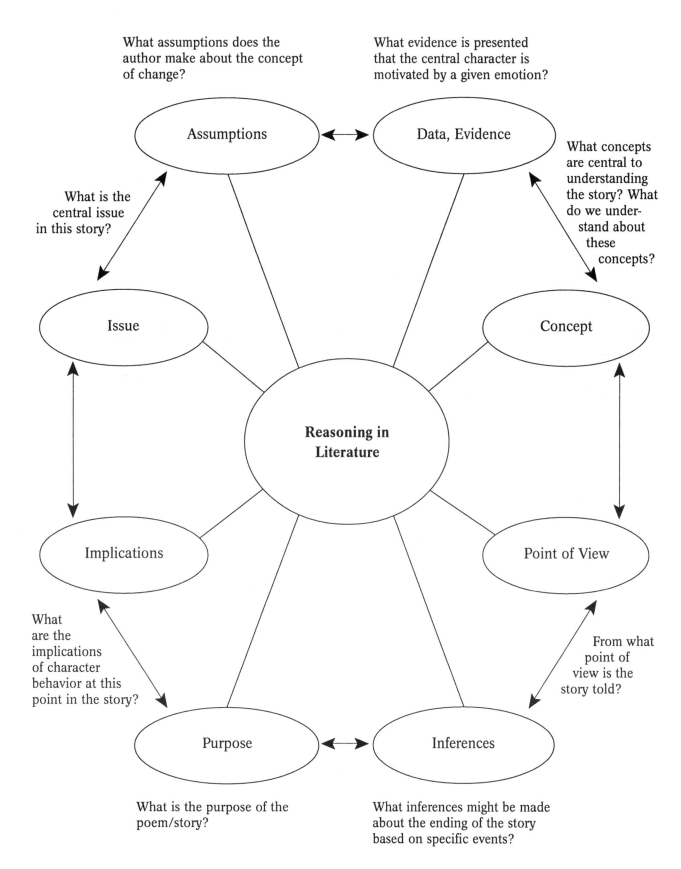

What assumptions does the author make about the concept of change?

What evidence is presented that the central character is motivated by a given emotion?

What concepts are central to understanding the story? What do we understand about these concepts?

What is the central issue in this story?

Assumptions

Data, Evidence

Issue

Concept

Reasoning in Literature

Implications

Point of View

What are the implications of character behavior at this point in the story?

From what point of view is the story told?

Purpose

Inferences

What is the purpose of the poem/story?

What inferences might be made about the ending of the story based on specific events?

▼ RESEARCH MODEL

The research model provides students with a way to approach an issue of significance and explore it individually and in small groups. Its organization follows major elements of reasoning. Teachers are encouraged to model each stage of this process in class. For specific lessons in teaching the research model, procure a copy of *A Guide to Teaching Research Skills and Strategies in Grades 4–12*, available for purchase from the Center for Gifted Education at the College of William and Mary.

---

1. **Identify your issue or problem.**

   What is the issue or problem?

   Who are the stakeholders and what are their positions?

   What is *your* position on this issue?

---

2. **Read about your issue and identify points of view or arguments through information sources.**

   What are my print sources?

   What are my media sources?

   What are my people sources?

   What are my preliminary findings based on a review of existing sources?

---

3. **Form a set of questions that can be answered by a specific set of data.**

Examples:

   A. What would be the results of _____?

   B. Who would benefit and by how much?

   C. Who would be harmed and by how much?

My research questions:

---

4. **Gather evidence through research techniques such as surveys, interviews, or experiments.**

What survey questions should I ask?

What interview questions should I ask?

What experiments should I do?

5. **Manipulate and transform data so they can be interpreted.**

How can I summarize what I found?

Should I develop charts, diagrams, or graphs to represent my data?

6. **Draw conclusions and make inferences.**

What does the data mean? How can I interpret what I found out?

How do the data support your original point of view?

How do they it support other points of view?

What conclusions do you make about the issue?

7. **Determine implications and consequences.**

What are the consequences of following the point of view that you support?

Do I know enough or are there now new questions to be answered?

8. **Communicate your findings. (Prepare an oral presentation for classmates based on note cards and written report.)**

What are my purpose, issue, and point of view, and how will I explain them?

What data will I use to support my point of view?

How will I conclude my presentation?

▼ C. Alignment of the Units with National Standards

These units of study have been aligned with the English standards developed by the National Council of Teachers of English (NCTE) and the International Reading Association (IRA). They respond well to all major aspects of those standards, while incorporating a rigorous assessment component to enhance individual student progress during and at the conclusion of each unit. The alignment process has also been done for individual state documents in language arts, including those of Connecticut, New York, South Carolina, Texas, and Virginia. Selected district alignments have also been completed.

The chart on the following page represents the NCTE/IRA alignment.

Alignment with NCTE/IRA Standards

Standards for the English Language Arts	William and Mary Language Arts Units
Students read a wide range of print and nonprint texts to build an understanding of texts, of themselves, and of the cultures of the United States and the world; to acquire new information; to respond to the needs and demands of society and the workplace; and for personal fulfillment.	Emphasis on multicultural and global literature and broad-based reading.
Students read a wide range of literature from many periods in many genres to build an understanding of the many dimensions (e.g., philosophical, ethical, aesthetic) of human experience.	Broad-based reading in poetry, short story, biography, essay, and novel forms.
Students apply a wide range of strategies to comprehend, interpret, evaluate, and appreciate texts.	Major goal on analysis and interpretation of literature. (Goal 1)
Students adjust their use of spoken, written, and visual language to communicate effectively with a variety of audiences and for different purposes.	Sensitivity to audience built into writing and research activities.
Students employ a wide range of strategies as they write and use different writing process elements appropriately.	Major outcome related to effective use of all stages of the writing process. (Goal 2)
Students apply knowledge of language structure, language conventions, media techniques, figurative language, and genre to create, critique, and discuss print and nonprint texts.	Major goal of developing linguistic competency. (Goal 3)
Students conduct research on issues and interests by generating ideas and questions and by posing problems. They gather, evaluate, and synthesize data from a variety of sources to communicate their discoveries in ways that suit their purpose and audience.	Research project that focuses on these skills based on issue identification is a feature of each unit; the use of the reasoning model underlies the teaching of all language arts strands. (Goal 5)
Students use a wide variety of technological and informational resources to gather and synthesize information and to create and communicate knowledge.	Incorporated in research model and writing task demands.
Students develop an understanding of and respect for diversity in language use, patterns, and dialects across cultures, ethnic groups, geographic regions, and social roles.	Applicable to the context of selected literature.
Students whose first language is not English make use of their first language to develop competency in the English language arts and understanding of content across the curriculum.	N/A
Students participate as knowledgeable, reflective, creative, and critical members of a variety of literacy communities.	Contact with authors, use of peer review, major discussions of literary works.
Students use spoken, written, and visual language to accomplish their own purposes.	Integrated throughout the units.

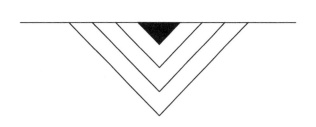

SECTION
IV

ASSESSING THE APPROPRIATENESS OF LANGUAGE ARTS CURRICULUM FOR YOUR SCHOOL DISTRICT

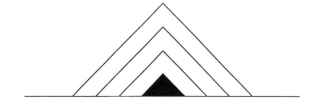

▼ A. Introduction and Rationale for Language Arts Curriculum Assessment

The task of assessing language arts curriculum for appropriateness becomes critical in the context of national reform. Several national organizations such as the International Reading Association and the National Council of Teachers of English have called for all language arts education to make fundamental changes both in content and in processes emphasized in material. Changing the factual and didactic orientation of the current curriculum and the materials that reinforce it to meet these new goals will require changing the very structures and foundations of the curriculum itself; a change in paradigm.

Two challenges are presented to reviewers of curricula who accept the validity and necessity of the "new curriculum" model. The first is to find a way to rate current curricula that is fair to the intent of the publishers and authors while attending to the assumption that in order to be effective, language arts instruction will follow a significantly new form. Basal texts which may be evaluated as perfectly sound under the old paradigm may in fact look less promising when rated using "new" standards. Nevertheless, such a review provides part of the demonstration of where and how changes need to be made to meet the demands of the 21st century.

The second challenge is to find a new and appropriate set of standards for determining differentiation for high-ability students. The National Language Arts standards document outlines literacy processes which should be cultivated in all American students (National Council of Teachers of English and International Reading Association, 1996). This list, while new to the goals of most general education programs, looks very much like the list of goals which teachers of the gifted have had for their students for some time. If all students should learn how to analyze and interpret literature, write persuasively, think productively, conduct research, and communicate well, then what will the new set of standards for gifted students be?

A good core curriculum is an essential foundation to exemplary language arts instruction. Because of the interest in engaging students in language arts over time, it has become increasingly important to select or create curriculum which simultaneously achieves several goals:

▼ The delivery of content which is substantive, technologically relevant, and essential to an understanding of the communication arts;

▼ The demonstration of practices and "habits of mind" to give students practice in the behavior and thinking of writers and how to be a productive member of a literary community;

▼ The delivery of content and processes in a context which excites and entices students without diminishing the value of the content or reducing the practice of teaching to games or "magic"; and

▼ The opportunity for students to make connections among the language arts areas of reading, writing, speaking and listening, and between language arts and other areas of study.

While such a core curriculum emphasis is essential for all learners, differentiating for the high-ability learner requires responding to the interests and behaviors displayed by these learners. Thus, high-ability learners need advanced content earlier and at a more complex and abstract level than do other learners, even given the new standards model.

Because curriculum materials are considered so crucial to the enterprise of teaching, we believe that the following set of criteria will prove valuable to school districts making decisions about materials in language arts. The users of the criteria may be (1) curriculum developers, (2) district-based curriculum or textbook review committees, or (3) individual teachers interested in materials for classroom use. We hope the process conveys a reasonable approach to decision-making about educational materials in language arts and that practitioners will find it helpful.

Overview of the Review Process

Our goals for curriculum review were: (1) to develop a comprehensive evaluation system that would provide a template for reviewing all language arts curriculum materials and (2) to generate curriculum reviews which would enable consumers to match available curricula with their locally identified needs. In order to reach these goals, we sought to conduct the following activities:

▼ to develop criteria by which a curriculum can be evaluated against a standard of excellence

▼ to develop comprehensive criteria that would assess curricula in three areas: curriculum design, exemplary language arts, and tailoring for special populations

▼ to create a system that would enable consumers to compare one set of materials to another

▼ to provide a multifaceted review of curricula that couples a numerical rating system with the personal reactions and insights of the reviewers

▼ to institute a collaborative review forum that incorporates the perspectives of a language arts specialist, curriculum development expert, and expert in materials

The review process illustrated in Figure 1 was designed as a collaborative endeavor that involved these varied specialists. The curriculum specialists' expertise included general curriculum development, specialized curriculum for gifted learners, and the areas of speech communication, writing, and the teaching of literature and reading. The reviewers' classroom experience ranged from preschool to graduate school. In addition, each of them had experience teaching gifted learners at the elementary level and developing curriculum. This group with primary review responsibility was supported by a consultant group of educators and scholars who provided information on current issues in language arts and state-of-the-art curriculum materials.

Developing Criteria

The development of criteria was the cornerstone of the entire review process. The review team worked together to identify significant criteria, define each criterion, and test the criteria on sample curriculum.

Figure 1

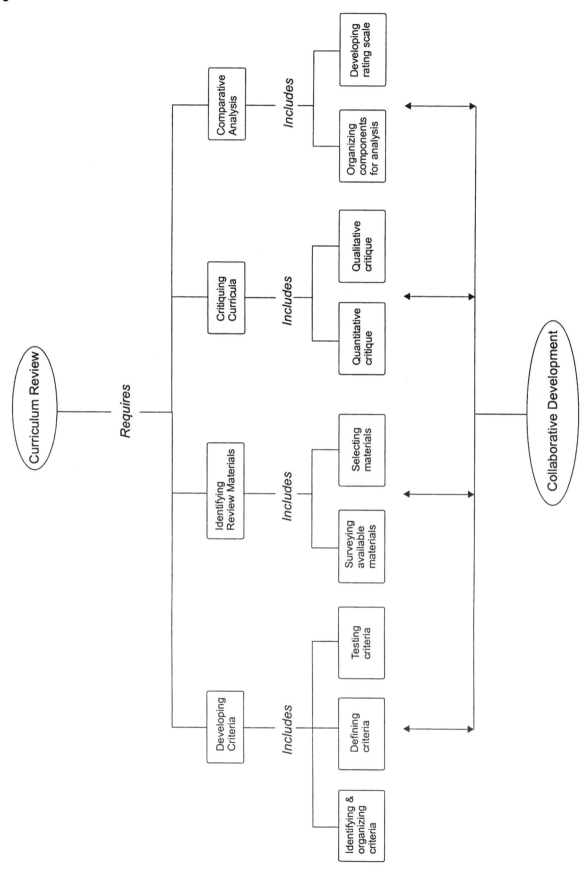

Identifying the criteria forced the team to consider the essential elements of curriculum, which coalesced into three categories:

1. Curriculum features: elements that enable teachers to plan, deliver and assess instruction
2. Exemplary language arts: elements of subject matter content and process
3. Special populations: elements addressing the needs and concerns of high-ability learners

The work of VanTassel-Baska and her colleagues (VanTassel-Baska, 1992; 1994; VanTassel-Baska, Johnson, & Boyce, 1996) provided the foundational set of criteria for effective curriculum features and development. Specifically, this set looked at instructional objectives and how those objectives could be attained through the careful organization of activities, strategies and materials, and then assessed. The criteria addressed issues that ranged from "use of various types of questions" to "developmental readiness."

Recent national reports in the language arts have called for a reconsideration of language arts curricula that use the best of classical and contemporary literature texts to teach language, writing, and literature through an inquiry-based approach (Suhor, 1984). Such reports also stress the importance of using such approaches throughout elementary and junior high school. Close and active reading of various genre is also encouraged, even at the expense of broad coverage (National Assessment Governing Board, 1992). Constructivist theory, as it is applied to the language arts, has focused on the importance of students' creating meaning from using literary sources, particularly in the writing process (Spivey, 1990). Other theorists view the province of teaching language arts as using the classical canon and teaching traditional forms of writing (Hirsch, 1987; Thompson, 1991). Accompanying modes of assessment have been developed that reflect intensive involvement with literary works, focusing more on the process of reading, the thought patterns of students engaged in it, and the power of thought brought to bear in connecting one work to another (National Assessment Governing Board, 1992). There exists, however, a significant gap between theory and practice. Researchers in literacy development generally have deplored the lack of curriculum research on testing what works in schools (Langer & Allington, 1992). One of the challenges, then is to find ways to incorporate ideas about literacy development and put them into "testable" practice in the schooling process.

Research on how students learn is also critical to consider in developing new curriculum. Learning is an interactive process that brings together the learner, an activity or task, and the situation that surrounds them (Novak & Gowin, 1984). Thus, there is concern for ensuring a "holistic view" in a language arts curriculum. A literate environment provides rewarding experiences in which students construct meaning for themselves in real situations. Students work collaboratively, using the teacher as a model. Learners engage in revising their work as a welcome part of their regular school experience. An integrated curriculum uses communication skills as interrelated processes that support each other and as enabling skills across all subject areas. Outcome-based curriculum goals focus on whole thinking processes that are at a sufficiently challenging conceptual level. A "thinking" curriculum requires awareness of one's thinking, including attitudes, habits, and dispositions, as well as the critical and creative thinking processes about ideas. Such language arts curriculum encourages and supports student responsibility for learning and encourages and supports student choice, collaboration, and active participation. Such a curriculum also needs to be aligned so that what is written is also taught and tested, allowing instruction and assessment to become interrelated areas.

All of the new directions suggested by the theory and research of those in the language arts community tend to focus on some common themes for language arts curriculum reform in schools. These themes include the following:

▼ Making the learner the centerpiece for constructing meaning, using open-ended inquiry as primary teaching tool

▼ Integrating the language arts areas

▼ Making connections to disciplines outside the language arts

▼ Setting learner outcomes at high levels

▼ Using authentic assessment

▼ Developing in students the skills, attitudes, and dispositions of good readers, writers and communicators

▼ Using literature that satisfies both classical and multicultural considerations

The special populations for whom specific criteria were developed included high-ability learners who were intellectually able and/or verbally talented. These criteria may be applied to the top 20 percent of the school age population. The work of VanTassel-Baska (1994) informed the criteria development for high-ability learners. The criteria emphasized acceleration and compression of content, higher order thinking in the language arts creation of real products, and the exploration of meaningful themes and ideas.

After the criteria were identified, the review team worked together to define terms. Finally, the team tested the criteria by applying them to various curricula and comparing each team member's ratings. The tests and ensuing discussions led to new definitions and to revisions of criteria. In addition, team members located superior and inferior examples of various criteria; these examples then served as benchmarks for evaluating other curricula.

▼ B. Why Schools Need to Review Language Arts Materials

In order for practitioners at all levels of education to make informed decisions about instruction, they must first become informed consumers. The model described here offers a way to examine current practices embedded in the materials we use in classrooms and to initiate change that is necessary for instructional improvement and educational reform.

The Review Process Enhances Decision Making

A collaborative review process is useful at all levels of instruction. At the classroom level, it enables teachers to make informed choices by providing the criteria to choose challenging materials for valid, worthy activities and the knowledge base to dismiss time-consuming distractions. At the school level, the collaborative review process provides principals and librarians with a vehicle for involving the entire staff in decision-making on materials acquisitions. At the system and state level, it adds rigor to the textbook adoption process. The process provides an in-depth, systematic way to compare one curriculum with another, and it illuminates the lack of research base for many of the heavily marketed, commercial curricula.

The Review Process Facilitates Collaboration

The process of collaborative curriculum review offers an ongoing model to examine what's working and what's not working for curriculum delivery within a local school or within a school system. Once a set of criteria become understood by a group and internalized, teachers and administrators have a method by which to improve instruction. In addition to defining terms and agreeing on standards, the process includes seeing another's perspective and tapping into another realm of expertise. The expertise within buildings, systems, and communities becomes available for meaningful, productive collaboration. Classroom teachers, subject specialists or experts in other fields, educators of special populations such as gifted learners and at-risk groups, guidance counselors and psychologists, librarians and media specialists all contribute different but essential knowledge and perspective. Collaborative review becomes a self-generating, learning process that results not just in a curriculum review but a heightened awareness of possibilities for effective classroom practice.

The Review Process Is Dynamic

To be effective and viable, the review process and model require constant revisiting. For example, new research on the learning process and the consideration of evolving technology must continue to be incorporated into the criteria. In essence, continually revising criteria is part of an informed consumer process and essential to intellectual life. It is a fundamental aspect of education and one that teachers need to impart to students.

One of the values of this review process is that it considers curriculum resources other than textbooks. Tulley and Farr (1990) argued, "As long as educators continue to assume that the textbook is the curriculum, teachers will be powerless to exert change" (p. 169). The review process makes it evident that alternative materials such as modular curricula combine content and process in more powerful ways than reading-based textbooks. The need for change becomes urgently clear when choices are seen in a broader context, thereby expanding the range of possibilities.

Instructional improvement and the restructuring of schools depends on a shared vision of various groups and disciplines. Collaborative review offers a way for groups to identify mutual goals, to determine the criteria for excellence, and to work together. The implications of this review process for effective collaboration combined with the possibilities for staff development and instructional improvement warrant serious consideration.

▼ C. Definitions of Criteria for Review

In the following section, the list of relevant criteria to consider in reviewing language arts curriculum materials is provided for all three phases of consideration. Each criterion is accompanied by a definition.

General Curriculum Features Evaluation Form
(Phase I Review)

Curriculum Design

1. *Rationale and Purpose*
   This feature addresses the reasons for developing a particular unit of study for use with a given group of learners at a particular stage of development. It provides the reader with a sense of the importance of the topic under study and why it is being taught.

   ▼ **Substantive and worthy**
   Content is important and valuable; publishers/authors provide reasons why content was selected or the value is self-evident.

   ▼ **Clear and understandable**
   Teachers can easily tell why the selected content is important. Rationale and purpose are written in meaningful and clear language rather than in educational jargon.

   ▼ **Logical order and integrated structure to scope and sequence**
   The suggested order for presentation of topics and concepts makes sense both within a grade and from grade to grade.

   ▼ **Identified outcomes consonant with purpose**
   The content and processes identified as desired goals of learning are consistent with the stated reasons to learn.

2. *Curriculum Content*
   This feature provides the scope of the unit in respect to content treatment and allows the reader to see the interrelationships of ideas that will guide the unit development process.

   ▼ **Significant concepts**
   The language arts content is central to fundamental understanding about a language arts content area and/or process.

   ▼ **Significant information to explore concepts in depth**
   Enough factual information should be provided to cover selected concepts in depth, as opposed to a cursory sampling of information across many concepts.

   ▼ **Topics support concepts**
   Individual areas of study in the curriculum illuminate/provide examples for larger, more abstract language arts concepts.

▼ **Engaging style of present information**
The material is attractive (well-illustrated, up-to-date, etc.), catches the attention of the learner, and engages the learner.

▼ **Topics and activities have personal meaning and social relevance for students**
Information is presented from a child's point of reference.

▼ **Allowance for curricular differentiation for gifted learners**
The possibility to adjust content level or pace and acceleration of the curriculum exists. Suggestions for such adaptations are provided.

3. *Curriculum Responsiveness to Developmental Needs*
This feature of the curriculum assures that there is an optimal match between the developmental readiness of the learner and the curricular expectations.

▼ **Sequential exposure to language arts concepts from the concrete to the abstract**
Depending on the age and/or grade level, the language arts ideas shift from being tangible with hands-on tasks and/or basic explanations to a more abstract and generalizable form.

▼ **Active engagement with language arts materials used to support the curriculum**
There are activities and resources available or suggested so that students can "do" language arts.

▼ **Sequential use of visual materials from the picto-centric to the text-centered**
Content is presented primarily through engaging and interesting picture books in early primary grades and moves to proportionately standard written text in higher grades.

Classroom Design

4. *Instructional Objectives*
This feature provides the focus and direction for learning in the unit. It specifies anticipated outcomes for students as a result of being taught a unit of study.

▼ **Clear and understandable**
A curriculum reader would know immediately what the students will be able to know and/or do as a result of a unit of study.

▼ **Measurable**
Techniques or suggestions are provided for teachers so they can tell whether or not they have achieved the learning outcomes.

▼ **Related to overall rationale and purpose**
The goals of an individual unit are consistent with the goals of the curriculum as a whole.

5. *Activities*
This feature specifies what teachers will do to facilitate learning and what students will do to learn.

▼ **Appropriate balance of teacher direction/student direction**
Room is provided in the curriculum both to meet teacher goals and to allow for students to participate and contribute to the class.

▼ **Developmentally appropriate activities**
The activities take into account the level of cognitive, emotional, and physical development that is likely to be found in learners who will be doing these activities. Activities are challenging, yet achievable.

▼ **Activities used to develop conceptual understanding**
The activities allow students to deepen their understanding of core language arts concepts.

▼ **Activities clarify, reinforce and extend content**
Activities serve a purpose related to learning content beyond repeating what students already know. They directly support the content-base of the unit.

▼ **Language arts integrated with other subjects**
Interdisciplinary connections are presented. Activities encourage exploration of the relationships between language arts and other subjects such as social studies, science, math, art, and music.

6. *Instructional Strategies*
This feature provides direction to readers around the major approaches to teaching that will be undertaken. It specifies teaching models, questioning techniques, and conferencing approaches used by the teacher.

▼ **Varied strategies**
Several different forms of instruction are suggested (e.g., inquiry activities, lecture, discussion, independent research, etc.)

▼ **Opportunities for problem finding and solving**
Students are encouraged to identify and solve problems that are not explicitly set out for them in advance.

▼ **Opportunities for open inquiry**
Projects that are issue-based or problem-based are open-ended with respect to the solution or the approach to the solution. Students are encouraged to formulate questions and explore possible answers to those questions.

▼ **Varied grouping approach, e.g., including opportunities for small group and independent work**
The curriculum suggests both large and small group activities and different ways these groups can be formed and used.

▼ **Cooperative work focused on sharing multiple perspectives on issues**
The process of sharing ideas is treated as more important than a single "right answer."

▼ **Opportunities to practice decision making strategies**
Students are encouraged to make decisions rather than have the teachers tell them all procedures and outcomes.

▼ **Use of various types of questions (e.g., convergent, divergent, evaluative)**
There are a variety of questions suggested which stimulate different levels of thought, from knowledge through evaluation.

7. *Assessment Procedures*

This feature specifies how students will be assessed in respect to their learning in the unit. It provides documentation for learning outcomes.

▼ **Presence of pre/post assessment measures**
There are opportunities at both the beginning and the end of the unit to measure knowledge so that relative gain can be measured.

▼ **Use of observational evaluation**
Opportunities for assessment by observation are included.

▼ **Use of authentic assessment**
There are opportunities for students to demonstrate their skills and growth through authentic language arts tasks such as writing, discussion, and oral presentation rather than only objective tests.

▼ **Objective attainment assessment measures**
There are evaluation strategies which measure directly whether or not the student has met an objective.

▼ **Assessment based on ability to get and to use information**
Assessment procedures require students to access and use information, rather than simply recognize facts.

▼ **Assessment based on outcomes of significance**
The objectives that are assessed are ones that are valuable and important to language arts concepts, processes, or attitudes.

▼ **Opportunity for overall evaluation**
Opportunity is provided for a holistic, integrated final evaluation. There is some way of assessing whether objectives for a whole unit or curriculum have been achieved.

8. *Materials/Resources*

This feature provides bibliographic references for use in implementing the unit. It includes both resources for teachers and materials for student use.

▼ **Instructional materials begin with students' current knowledge**
The materials provide for diagnostic assessment of knowledge and skills and/or introductory activities that encourage teacher assessment of knowledge levels.

▼ **Supportive bibliography for teachers**
Resources are suggested for teachers to enhance their knowledge of the subject.

▼ **Frequent student misconceptions are identified for teachers**
Teachers are alerted to what errors or pitfalls students commonly make or experience.

▼ **Bibliography for student extension reading**
Bibliographies are provided for the learners.

▼ **Supportive handout materials (informational, worksheets, etc.)**
Materials are included that are ready for duplication and that support the basic curriculum unit.

9. *Extension Ideas*

This feature specifies follow-up learning opportunities for students that go beyond the prepared unit of study but are logical next activities, based on unit work. Suggestions for both group and independent work should be encouraged.

▼ **Worthwhile, related activities for students to pursue independently**
Meaningful suggestions are included for ways a student can extend the school learning experience to the home environment. Ideas, activities, and resources are suggested so the individual student can do extended work on a given topic, concept, or theme.

10. *Technology Features**

This set of features specifies the extent to which the technology aspect of the curriculum is appropriate and effective in enhancing language arts learning experiences.

General

▼ **Actively engages students in higher order thinking skills and activities**

▼ **Enhances and complements instruction**

▼ **Provides effective interaction**

▼ **Allows exploration otherwise prohibited by time or money**

▼ **Provides access to resources that are unavailable in print, timely, or more comprehensive than media center printed materials**

▼ **Contains several levels of difficulty**

▼ **Provides useful, corrective feedback**

▼ **Easy to use**

Technical

▼ **Uncluttered screen design**

▼ **Lucid, economical text**

▼ **Dynamic visuals for abstract concepts**

▼ **Useful help screens**

▼ **Effective self-pacing devices**

▼ **Comprehensive teacher manual that includes instructions for use and modification, inventory, and specifications**

---

* This feature was not rated if the curriculum materials did not include it.

Exemplary Language Arts Features Evaluation Form
(Phase II Review)

1. *Reading/Literature*

   ▼ **Choice of literature**

   The choice of literature or reading material is based on intellectual, affective, and multi-cultural considerations.

   ▼ **Critical reading**

   The unit emphasizes expectations for critical reading behaviors.

   ▼ **Textual analysis**

   The unit incorporates textual analysis of conceptually rich primary source material.

2. *Multiculturalism/Globalism*

   ▼ **Quality of material**

   The unit incorporates the best of multicultural literature and related materials.

   ▼ **Balanced perspective**

   There is a balanced perspective on at least three diverse cultures.

   ▼ **Contributions of various cultural groups embedded**

   The contributions of various cultural groups are embedded rather than treated separately.

3. *Writing*

   ▼ **Concept mapping**

   The materials use concept mapping to teach outlining.

   ▼ **Emphasis on different types of writing**

   The materials emphasize different kinds of, including descriptive, narrative, persuasive, expository, and technical.

   ▼ **Use of writing strategies**

   The materials focus on strategies for developing a thesis statement, providing supportive evidence, and drafting a conclusion.

   ▼ **Use of revision**

   The materials reflect the use of revision in the writing process.

   ▼ **Use of workshopping techniques**

   The materials reflect the use of workshopping techniques (such as peer review and discussion of each other's writing).

4. *Language Study*

   ▼ **Word relationships**

   The materials emphasize the development of word relationships, such as synonyms, antonyms, and analogies.

▼ **Vocabulary development**

The materials include opportunities to learn appropriate level advanced vocabulary.

▼ **Linguistic competence**

The materials encourage the development of linguistic competence in English, with emphasis on grammatical structure.

▼ **History of language**

The materials include opportunities to learn about the history of language, etymology, and/or semantics.

▼ **Mechanics and usage**

The materials provide a review of basic mechanics needed to communicate, such as capitalization and punctuation.

5. *Speaking/Listening Communication*

▼ **Active engagement**

The materials provide opportunities for students to engage in active speaking and listening activities.

▼ **Opportunities for making oral presentations**

The materials provide opportunities for students to engage in various forms of oral expression, including dramatic presentations, persuasive speeches, and debate.

▼ **Causation**

The materials promote involvement of students in responding to each other's presentations through questions, discussion, and critique.

▼ **Critical thinking**

The materials address critical thinking skills through listening and speaking.

6. *Research Process*

▼ **Provision of a model**

The students are directly taught a research model.

▼ **Issue/problem generation**

Alternatives are provided for students to develop their own issues.

▼ **Development of research questions**

Students are encouraged to participate in/develop researchable questions.

▼ **Broad-based communication**

Opportunities for research work that can be shared with multiple audiences are provided.

Differentiation for High-Ability Learners

1. **Provisions for acceleration and compression of content**
   Curriculum skills and concepts are organized on a sequence from "easy to difficult" concepts that would allow for easy teacher adaptation to students' individual instructional levels.

2. **Use of higher order thinking skills**
   The curriculum includes activities and questions that require learners to think at the levels of analysis, synthesis, and evaluation.

3. **Integration of content by key ideas, issues, and themes**
   The curriculum is organized according to broad-based concepts in language arts, such as change, patterns, and systems.

4. **Connection of ideas to other disciplines**
   The curriculum illustrates how language arts ideas have salience in other content areas such as music, art, social studies, and mathematics.

5. **Opportunities for advanced and broad-based reading**
   The curriculum provides students selected activities and materials that are sufficiently challenging and interdisciplinary for advanced learners.

6. **Use of multiple teaching resources**
   The curriculum encourages the use of multiple media, multiple readings, and multiple activities from other materials to teach skills and concepts.

7. **Use of diagnostic-prescriptive teaching**
   The curriculum provides an assessment approach that allows for pre-testing and post-testing as well as on-going assessment of learners' mastery of skills and concepts.

8. **Attention to instructional pacing**
   The teachers' guide notes that some learners can master the basic language arts content at a rate faster than other learners.

9. **Advanced reading level**
   The curriculum readability index is pitched at least one or two grade levels beyond the given designated level.

10. **Opportunities for students to develop advanced products**
    The curriculum provides suggestions for teachers to support student projects that involve original investigation.

11. **Opportunities for independent learning based on student ability and interest**
    The curriculum provides extension activities to be undertaken by students alone in various settings.

12. **Use of inquiry-based instructional techniques**
    The curriculum is based on a model of questioning that promotes the role of the student as investigator.

▼ D. Procedures for Using the Curriculum Assessment Forms

1. Select a review team composed of teachers, administrators, and specialists with expertise in general curriculum, language arts curriculum, and curriculum for high-ability learners. Remember to include your library media specialist as a part of this group. A review team should not exceed 6–8 individuals.

2. Read and review the Curriculum Assessment forms as a group, especially the review forms and the underlying definitions for the criteria presented in them.

3. Collect materials for team review.

4. Assign your most experienced reviewers to rate all three phases (no more than two individuals). Then assign each of the remaining reviewers the phase that corresponds best to their expertise. At least two reviews should be done for each individual phase.

5. Use the accompanying review forms for this process.

6. Compile data across reviewers on the overall rating form and hold a team session to discuss reviews according to the specific material reviewed.

7. Make materials selection decisions based on a) the match between the materials and the goals and objectives of your district language arts program, b) the match with district needs for supplementary materials, and c) the match with special population needs.

▼ E. CURRICULUM ASSESSMENT OVERALL RATING FORM

The Curriculum Assessment Overall Rating Form found below provides a model for synthesizing the key features evaluated for each set of curriculum materials reviewed. The numerical average of reviewed ratings for each feature may be transferred onto this single sheet so that rating recommendations might be made according to individual features of the curriculum. For example, some curricula may be very strong in language arts and thus recommended for that feature. The same curricula may be found inadequate in general curriculum features and thus not recommended based on that set of criteria. The purpose and function of this rating form, then, is to provide a shorthand coding for the results of the multi-layered review process.

The Curriculum Assessment Overall Rating Form

	Phase I: General Curriculum Features	Phase II: Exemplary Language Arts Features	Phase III: Tailoring for High-Ability Learners	Notes
Reviewer 1				
Reviewer 2				
Reviewer 3				
Reviewer 4				
Reviewer 5				
Reviewer 6				
Reviewer 7				
Reviewer 8				

▼ F. THE CURRICULUM ASSESSMENT FORMS

General Curriculum Features
Phase I

Name of Reviewer: _____

Title: _____

Title of Curriculum to Be Reviewed: _____

Appropriate Grade Level(s): _____ Original Copyright Date: _____

Date(s) of Revision: _____

Directions: Carefully read through all curriculum materials and then rate the curriculum by each of the following criteria on a scale of 5 = To an exemplary extent; 4 = To a good extent; 3 = Adequate; 2 = To a limited extent; and 1 = Not at all.

1. *Rationale and Purpose*
   —Substantive and worthy   5   4   3   2   1
   —Clear and understandable   5   4   3   2   1
   —Logical order and integrated structure to scope and
      sequence   5   4   3   2   1
   —Identified outcomes consonant with purpose   5   4   3   2   1

2. *Curriculum Content*
   —Significant concepts   5   4   3   2   1
   —Significant information to explore concepts in depth   5   4   3   2   1
   —Topics support concepts   5   4   3   2   1
   —Engaging style of present information   5   4   3   2   1
   —Topics and activities have personal meaning and social
      relevance for students   5   4   3   2   1
   —Allowance for curriculum differentiation for gifted learners   5   4   3   2   1

3. *Curriculum Responsiveness to Developmental Needs*
   —Sequential exposure to language arts concepts from the
      concrete to the abstract   5   4   3   2   1
   —Active engagement with language arts materials used
      to support the curriculum   5   4   3   2   1
   —Sequential use of visual materials from the picto-centric
      to the text centered   5   4   3   2   1

4. *Instructional Objectives*

—Clear and understandable	5	4	3	2	1
—Measurable	5	4	3	2	1
—Related to overall rationale and purpose	5	4	3	2	1

5. *Activities*

—Appropriate balance of teacher direction/student direction	5	4	3	2	1
—Developmentally appropriate activities	5	4	3	2	1
—Activities used to develop conceptual understanding	5	4	3	2	1
—Activities clarify, reinforce, and extend content	5	4	3	2	1
—Language arts integrated with other subjects	5	4	3	2	1

6. *Instructional Strategies*

—Varied strategies	5	4	3	2	1
—Opportunities for problem finding and solving	5	4	3	2	1
—Opportunities for open inquiry	5	4	3	2	1
—Varied grouping approaches including opportunities for small group and independent work	5	4	3	2	1
—Cooperative work focused on sharing multiple perspectives on issues	5	4	3	2	1
—Opportunities to practice decision-making strategies	5	4	3	2	1
—Use of various types of questions (e.g., convergent, divergent, evaluative)	5	4	3	2	1

7. *Assessment Procedures*

—Presence of pre/post assessment measures	5	4	3	2	1
—Use of observational evaluation	5	4	3	2	1
—Use of authentic assessment	5	4	3	2	1
—Objective attainment assessment measures	5	4	3	2	1
—Assessment based on ability to get and use information	5	4	3	2	1
—Assessment based on outcomes of significance	5	4	3	2	1
—Opportunity for overall evaluation	5	4	3	2	1

8. *Materials/Resources*

—Instructional materials begin with students' current knowledge	5	4	3	2	1
—Supportive bibliography for teachers	5	4	3	2	1
—Frequent student misconceptions are identified for teachers	5	4	3	2	1
—Bibliography for student extension reading	5	4	3	2	1
—Supportive handout materials (informational worksheets, etc)	5	4	3	2	1

9. *Extension Ideas*
   —Worthwhile, related activities for students to pursue
     independently   5   4   3   2   1

10. *Technology (if applicable)*
   —Actively engages students in higher order thinking
     skills and activities   5   4   3   2   1
   —Enhances and complements instruction   5   4   3   2   1
   —Provides effective interaction   5   4   3   2   1
   —Allows exploration otherwise prohibited by time or
     money   5   4   3   2   1
   —Provides access to resources that are unavailable in
     print, timely, or more comprehensive than media center
     printed materials   5   4   3   2   1
   —Contains several levels of difficulty   5   4   3   2   1
   —Provides useful, corrective feedback   5   4   3   2   1
   —Easy to use   5   4   3   2   1
   —Uncluttered screen design   5   4   3   2   1
   —Lucid, economical text   5   4   3   2   1
   —Dynamic visuals for abstract concepts   5   4   3   2   1
   —Useful help screens   5   4   3   2   1
   —Effective self-pacing devices   5   4   3   2   1
   —Comprehensive teacher manual that includes instructions
     for use and modification, inventory, and specifications   5   4   3   2   1

Overall average score for Phase I review:

Comments on strengths/weaknesses:

Exemplary Language Arts Features
Phase II

Name of Reviewer: _____

Title: _____

Title of Curriculum to Be Reviewed: _____

Appropriate Grade Level(s): _____ Original Copyright Date: _____

Date(s) of Revision: _____

Directions: Carefully read through all curriculum materials and then rate the curriculum by each of the following criteria on a scale of 5 = To an exemplary extent; 4 = To a good extent; 3 = Adequate; 2 = To a limited extent; and 1 = Not at all.

1. *Reading/Literature*
   —Choice of literature   5   4   3   2   1
   —Critical reading   5   4   3   2   1
   —Textual analysis   5   4   3   2   1

2. *Multiculturalism/Globalism*
   —Quality of material   5   4   3   2   1
   —Balanced perspective   5   4   3   2   1
   —Contributions of various cultural groups embedded   5   4   3   2   1

3. *Writing*
   —Concept mapping   5   4   3   2   1
   —Emphasis on different types of writing   5   4   3   2   1
   —Use of writing strategies   5   4   3   2   1
   —Use of revision   5   4   3   2   1
   —Use of workshopping techniques   5   4   3   2   1

4. *Language Study*
   —Word relationships   5   4   3   2   1
   —Vocabulary development   5   4   3   2   1
   —Linguistic competence   5   4   3   2   1
   —History of language   5   4   3   2   1
   —Mechanics and usage   5   4   3   2   1

5. *Speaking/Listening Communication*
   —Active engagement   5   4   3   2   1
   —Opportunities for making oral presentations   5   4   3   2   1
   —Causation   5   4   3   2   1
   —Critical thinking   5   4   3   2   1

6. *Research Process*

—Provision of a model	5	4	3	2	1
—Issue/problem generation	5	4	3	2	1
—Development of research questions	5	4	3	2	1
—Broad-based communication	5	4	3	2	1

Overall average score for Phase II review:

Comments on strengths/weaknesses:

Tailoring for Special Populations
Phase III

Name of Reviewer: _____

Title: _____

Title of Curriculum to Be Reviewed: _____

Appropriate Grade Level(s): _____

Although curriculum may be found exemplary from a technical and even subject area perspective, it is important to consider the extent to which curriculum can be tailored to the needs of more targeted groups of learners with special needs. Thus the Phase III review process looks more closely at the features of exemplary curriculum for special populations.

Directions: Carefully re-read through all curriculum materials and then, rate the curriculum by each of the following criteria on a scale of 5 = To an exemplary extent; 4 = To a good extent; 3 = Adequate; 2 = To a limited extent; and 1 = Not at all.

Differentiation for High-Ability Learners

1. Provisions for acceleration and compression of content	5	4	3	2	1
2. Use of higher order thinking skills	5	4	3	2	1
3. Integration of content by key ideas, issues, and themes	5	4	3	2	1
4. Connection of ideas to other disciplines	5	4	3	2	1
5. Opportunities for advanced and broad-based reading	5	4	3	2	1
6. Use of multiple teaching resources	5	4	3	2	1
7. Use of diagnostic-prescriptive teaching	5	4	3	2	1
8. Attention to instructional pacing	5	4	3	2	1
9. Advanced reading level	5	4	3	2	1
10. Opportunities for students to develop advanced products	5	4	3	2	1
11. Opportunities for independent learning based on student ability and interest	5	4	3	2	1
12. Use of inquiry-based instructional techniques	5	4	3	2	1

Overall average score for Phase III Review:

Comments on strengths/weaknesses:

▼ REFERENCES

Hirsch, E. D., Jr. (1987). *Cultural literacy: What every American needs to know.* Boston, MA: Houghton Mifflin.

Johnson, D., Boyce, L. N., & VanTassel-Baska, J. (1995). Evaluating curriculum materials in science. *Gifted Child Quarterly, 89,* 35–43.

Langer, J., & Allington, R. (1992). Curriculum research in writing and reading. In P. Jackson (Ed.), *Handbook of research on curriculum* (pp. 687–725). New York: Macmillan.

National Assessment Governing Board. (1992). *Reading framework for 1992 National Assessment of Education Progress.* Washington, DC: United States Department of Education.

National Council of Teachers of English and International Reading Association. (1996). *Standards for the English language arts.* Urbana, IL & Newark, DE: Authors.

Novak, J. D., & Gowin, D. B. (1984). *Learning how to learn.* New York: Cambridge University Press.

Spivey, N. (1990). Transforming texts. *Written Communication, 7,* 256–287.

Suhor, C. (1984). *1984 Report on trends and issues in English: A summary of reports from the NCTE commissions.* (ERIC Document Reproduction Service N. ED 239290.)

Thompson, M. (1991). *The magic lens.* Unionville, NY: Trillium.

Tulley, M., & Farr, R. (1990). Textbook evaluation and selection. In D. L. Elliott and A. Woodward (Eds.), *Textbooks and Schooling in the United States: Eighty-ninth Yearbook of the National Society for the Study of Education, Part I* (pp. 162–177). Chicago: The National Society for the Study of Education, distributed by the University of Chicago Press.

VanTassel-Baska, J. (1992). *Planning effective curriculum for gifted learners.* Denver: Love.

VanTassel-Baska, J. (Ed.) (1994). *Comprehensive curriculum for gifted learners* (2nd ed). Boston: Allyn & Bacon.

VanTassel-Baska, J., Johnson, D. T., & Boyce, L. N. (Eds). (1996). *Developing verbal talent.* Boston: Allyn & Bacon.

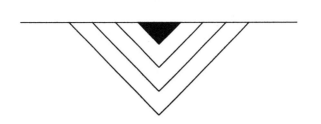

SECTION
V

SUPPORT STRUCTURES
FOR SUCCESSFUL
IMPLEMENTATION

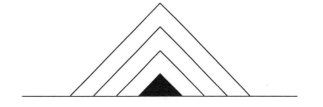

Teachers implementing these language arts units need to feel that they have the support necessary to make their teaching successful. Several areas of support are critical to making unit implementation work smoothly.

Administrative Support

Teachers must feel that their principals support them in the implementation process. Ways for principals to show support include

- ▼ attending workshops on the units with teachers
- ▼ observing teachers in the classroom (see checklist at end of section)
- ▼ holding periodic conferences with teachers to discuss implementation
- ▼ carrying on a discussion group on unit implementation that meets monthly

Materials Support

Teachers need to know that they can purchase and procure necessary materials for optimal implementation of the unit. Materials necessary include multiple copies of novels, *American Heritage* dictionaries, and related classroom resources. Ways for schools to provide materials support include

- ▼ asking the school librarian to order resource materials on a cost-sharing basis with other funding
- ▼ ordering and delivery of materials done by a central office coordinator
- ▼ materials procurement done by the principal and her staff

Teacher to Teacher Support

Many teachers benefit from having others in the same building to talk with about an innovation. Some ways this effort can be supported include

- ▼ holding teacher meetings to discuss curriculum implementation
- ▼ videotaping lessons for discussion
- ▼ having teachers observe each other and discuss what they saw
- ▼ developing a mentor teacher or cognitive coaching program to encourage instructional dialogue

Technology Support

Teachers implementing these units would benefit from having well integrated technology capabilities in their classroom. Ideally, each classroom would have access to computers with CD-ROM capability, e-mail, and Internet connections. Software programs should include word processing, drawing, and spreadsheet options. Specific software recommendations are included for specific units of study.

Final words to teacher implementers:

1. The units have been organized in a highly integrative way. Please try to implement them as fully as possible.

2. Teachers report that the units require "teacher learning" in order to be implemented effectively. Put in the time *before* beginning to teach the unit so that your students benefit optimally from the unit experience.

3. New teachers report great success in using the lesson plans because they are sufficiently detailed without being scripted. Use the material already prepared for you when possible.

4. Remember that change is challenging . . . but also necessary for growth and development. Enjoy the rigor and challenge!

Just as implementation ideas for a new curriculum are important to share with teachers, it is equally important to ensure that a system for monitoring language arts classrooms exists that documents the nature of the language arts learning going on. It is recommended that the attached *Classroom Indicators of Quality Instruction* checklist be used by appropriate educational personnel to determine the extent of implementation occurring in the classrooms. Principals, language arts coordinators, instructional leaders in schools may employ the form to assess the success of language arts reform recommendations.

▼ Classroom Indicators of Quality Instruction

Do our language arts classrooms contain the following elements?

Yes   No

____ ____ 1. Curriculum focuses on important concepts (e.g., systems, change, patterns, models).

____ ____ 2. Curriculum emphasizes the research process within an integrated framework (e.g., exploring a topic, planning and carrying out a study, judging results, and reporting).

____ ____ 3. Curriculum focuses on substantive content.

____ ____ 4. Instruction is inquiry-oriented, using strategies such as discussion and higher level questioning.

____ ____ 5. Instruction is activity-based, engaging students in active learning.

____ ____ 6. Assessment of learning includes performance-based approaches for students to demonstrate understanding and transfer of key ideas and processes.

____ ____ 7. Assessment of learning includes a portfolio of student work including formal writing assignments, response journal entries, reports, and other work.

____ ____ 8. Students engage in planning and carrying out original research.

____ ____ 9. Students demonstrate reasoning processes in their oral and written world. (*Teachers ask questions in classroom discussion and activities.*)

____ ____ 10. Students demonstrate reasoning processes in their oral and written work. (*Teachers ask reasoning questions in classroom discussion and activities.*)

____ ____ 11. The reading materials used are appropriate for different ability levels and employ various approaches to learning.

____ ____ 12. Classroom instruction incorporates appropriate technology as a tool in learning.

____ ____ 13. Classroom instruction attends to individual differences in rate of learning as evidenced by the use of learning centers, small group work, or individually differentiated work.

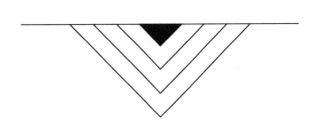

SECTION

VI

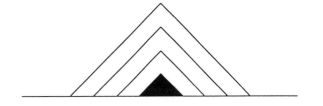

LANGUAGE ARTS RESOURCES FOR TEACHERS

▼ LANGUAGE ARTS RESOURCES FOR TEACHERS

American heritage dictionary of the English language (3rd ed). (1992). Boston: Houghton Mifflin.

Anders, G., & Beech, L. W. (1990). *Reading: Mapping for meaning.* New York: Sniffen Court Books.

Anderson, P. S., & Lapp, D. (1988). *Language skills in elementary education.* New York: Macmillan.

Appel, A., Jr. (1992). *The art of celebration: Twentieth-century painting, literature, sculpture, photography, and jazz.* New York: Alfred A. Knopf.

Barth, J. L., & Shermis, S. S. (1981). *Teaching social studies to the gifted and talented.* Indianapolis, IN: Indiana State Department of Public Instruction; Lafayette, IN: Purdue University Division of Curriculum. (ED 212118)

Baskin, B. H., & Harris, K. H. (1980). *Books for the gifted child.* New York: Bowker.

Bishop, R. S. (1987). Extending multicultural understanding through children's books. In B. E. Cullinan (Ed.), *Children's literature in the reading program* (pp. 60–67). Newark, DE: International Reading Association.

Bonafoux, P. (1985). *Portraits of the artist: The self-portrait in painting.* New York: Rizzoli.

Boyce, L. N. (1997). *A guide to teaching research skills and strategies in grades 4–12.* Williamsburg, VA: Center for Gifted Education.

Bradbury, R. (1990). *Zen and the art of writing.* Santa Barbara, CA: Capra Press.

Burkhalter, N. (1995). A Vygotsky-based curriculum for teaching persuasive writing in the elementary grades. *Language Arts, 72,* 192–196.

Chaney, A. L. (1992, June). *Issues in contemporary oral communication instruction.* Paper presented at the Language Arts Summer Institute, College of William and Mary, Williamsburg, VA.

Comber, G., Maistrellis, N., & Zeiderman, H. (1995). *Touchstones: Texts for discussion* (3rd ed.). Annapolis, MD: CZM Press.

Costa, A. L. (Ed.). (1991). *Developing minds.* (Rev. ed., Vol. 1–2) Alexandria, VA: Association for Supervision and Curriculum Development.

Dallas Museum of Art. (1989). *Ancestral legacy: The African impulse in African-American art.* Dallas, TX: Author.

Derwin, S., & Mills, C. (1988). *Introduction to the classics.* Baltimore, MD: Johns Hopkins University, Center for Talented Youth.

Elliot, E. (Ed.). (1991). *American literature: A Prentice Hall anthology.* Englewood, NJ: Prentice Hall.

Feder, N. (1965). *American Indian art.* New York: Harry N. Abrams.

Frank, M. (1987). *Complete writing lessons for the middle grades.* Nashville, TN: Incentive.

Furst, P. T., & Furst, J. L. (1982). *North American Indian art.* New York: Rizzoli.

Gallo, D. R. (Ed.). (1990). *Speaking for ourselves: Autobiographical sketches by notable authors of books for young adults.* Urbana, IL: National Council of Teachers of English.

Gallo, D. R. (Ed.). (1993). *Speaking for ourselves, too: More autobiographical sketches by notable authors of books for young adults*. Urbana, IL: National Council of Teachers of English.

Ganapole, S. J. (1989). Designing an integrated curriculum for gifted learners: An organizational framework. *Roeper Review, 12*, 81–86.

Gentile, C. (1992). *Exploring new methods for collecting students' school-based writing: NAEP's 1990 portfolio study*. Washington, DC: U.S. Government Printing Office.

Glen, D. (1990). Women who have made changes. *Challenge, 8*(5), 14–18.

Goodrich, F., & Hackett, A. (1985). *Enjoying literature*. New York: Macmillan.

Great Books Foundation. (1992). *An introduction to shared inquiry* (3rd. ed.). Chicago: Author.

Hall, D. (Ed.). (1985). *The Oxford book of children's verse in America*. New York: Oxford University Press.

Halsted, J. W. (1988). *Guiding gifted readers: From preschool through high school*. Columbus, OH: Ohio Psychology Press.

Halsted, J. W. (1994). *Some of my best friends are books*. Columbus, OH: Ohio Psychology Press.

Harris, V. J. (Ed.). (1992). *Teaching multicultural literature in grades K–8*. Norwood, MA: Christopher-Gordon.

Hauser, P., & Nelson, G. A. (1988). *Books for the gifted child, volume 2*. New York: Bowker.

Henderson, K. (1988). *Market guide for young writers*. Belvidere, NJ: Shoe Tree Press.

Highwater, J. (1978). *Many smokes, many moons: A chronology of American Indian history through Indian art*. Philadelphia: J. B. Lippincott Company.

Highwater, J. (1983). *Arts of the Indian Americans: Leaves from the sacred tree*. New York: Harper & Row.

Hirschberg, S. (1992). *One world many cultures*. New York: Macmillan.

Howard, K. (1990, Spring). Making the writing portfolio real. *The Quarterly of the National Writing Project and the Center for the Study of Writing and Literacy, 12*(2), pp. 4–7.

Howard, N. (1992). The unexpected. In J. VanTassel-Baska (Ed.), *Planning effective curriculum and instruction for gifted learners* (pp. 335–348). Denver, CO: Love.

Janeczko, P. B. (Ed.). (1990). *The place my W*O*R*D*S are looking for: What poets say about and through their work*. Scarsdale, NY: Bradbury.

Junyk, M. (1992). Women in literature. *Educational Oasis, 7*(4), 33–36.

Kaufer, D. S., Geisler, C. D., & Neuwirth, C. M. (1989). *Arguing from sources*. New York: Harcourt Brace Jovanovich.

Kennedy, C. (1994). *Teaching with writing: The state of the art*. In Center for Gifted Education (Ed.), *Language Arts Topics Papers*. Williamsburg, VA: Center for Gifted Education, College of William and Mary.

Kennedy, X. J., Kennedy, D. M., & Weinhaus, K. A. (1982). *Knock at a star: A child's introduction to poetry*. Boston: Little, Brown.

Koch, K., & Farrell, K. (Eds.). (1985). *Talking to the sun: An illustrated anthology of poems for young people*. New York: Henry Holt.

Langrehr, J. (1988). *Teaching students to think.* Bloomington, IN: National Education Service.

Levine, E. (1989). *I hate English!* New York: Scholastic.

Lipson, G. B., & Greenberg, B. N. (1981). *Extra! Extra! Read all about it: How to use the newspaper in the classroom.* Carthage, IL: Good Apple.

Lipson, G. B., & Romatowski, J. A. (1983). *Ethnic pride.* Carthage, IL: Good Apple.

Lucas, S. E. (1986). *The art of public speaking.* New York: Random House.

Marzano, R. J. (1992). *Cultivating thinking in English.* Urbana, IL: National Council of Teachers of English.

Marzano, R. J., Pickering, D. J., Arrendondo, D. E., Blackburn, G. J., Brandt, R. S., & Moffett, C. A. (1992). *Dimensions of learning: Teacher's manual.* Alexandria, VA: Association for Supervision and Curriculum Development.

Mattingley, R. (1992). Create a classroom of playwrights. *Challenge, 10*(4), 58–61.

Miller, R. K. (1992). *The informed argument: A multidisciplinary reader and guide* (3rd ed.). Fort Worth, TX: Harcourt Brace Jovanovich.

Miller-Lachmann, L. (1992). *Our family, our friends, our world: An annotated guide to significant multicultural books for children and teenagers.* New Providence, NJ: Bowker.

Minn, L. B. (1982). *Teach speech: Oral presentation strategies.* Carthage, IL: Good Apple.

Molloy, P. (Ed.) (1968). *Poetry U.S.A.* New York: Scholastic.

National Assessment Governing Board. (1992). *Reading framework for the 1992 National Assessment of Educational Progress.* Washington, DC: U.S. Government Printing Office.

National Center for Education Statistics. (1992). *National assessment of educational progress's 1990 portfolio study.* Washington, DC: U.S. Department of Education.

National Museum of Women in the Arts. (1987). *Women in the arts.* New York: Harry N. Abrams.

Norton, D. E. (1982). Using a webbing process to develop children's literature units. *Language Arts, 59,* 348–356.

Novak, J. D., & Gowin, D. B. (1984). *Learning how to learn.* New York: Cambridge University Press.

Olson, C. B. (1991). The thinking/writing connection. In A. L. Costa (Ed.), *Developing minds: A resource book for teaching thinking* (pp. 147–152). Alexandria, VA: Association for Supervision and Curriculum Development.

Page, C. H. (Undated). *The chief American poets.* New York: Houghton Mifflin.

Parnes, S. J. (1975). *Aha! Insights into creative behavior.* Buffalo, NY: DOK Publishers.

Paul, R., Binker, A. J. A., Jensen, K., & Kreklau, H. (1990). *Critical thinking handbook: 4th–6th grades, a guide for remodeling lesson plans in language arts, social studies, and science.* Rohnert Park, CA: Sonoma State University, Foundation for Critical Thinking.

Paul, R. (1992). *Critical thinking: What every person needs to survive in a rapidly changing world.* Sonoma, CA: The Foundation for Critical Thinking.

Plotz, H. (Ed.). (1977). *The gift outright: America to her poets.* New York: Greenwillow.

Polette, N. (1984). *The research book for gifted programs.* O'Fallon, MO: Book Lures.

Potter, R. R., & Goodman, R. B. (1983). *The world anthology.* New York: Globe.

Purves, A. C., Rogers, T., & Soter, A. O. (1990). *How porcupines make love II: Teaching a response-centered literature curriculum*. New York: Longman.

Ravitch, D. (Ed.). (1990). *The American reader: Words that moved a nation*. New York: HarperCollins.

Roalf, P. (1993). *Looking at paintings: Self-portraits*. New York: Hyperion.

Rottenberg, A. T. (1991). *Elements of argument: A text and reader* (3rd ed.). Boston: Bedford Books of St. Martin's Press.

Ryan, M. (1987). *So you have to give a speech!* New York: Franklin Watts.

Sandburg, C. (1992). *Selected poems*. New York: Gramercy.

Sebranek, P., Meyer, V., & Kemper, D. (1990). *Write source 2000*. Burlington, WI: Write Source Educational Publishing.

Seiger-Ehrenberg, S. (1985). Concept development. In A. L. Costa (Ed.), *Developing minds: A resource book for teaching thinking*. Alexandria, VA: Association for Supervision and Curriculum Development.

Shapiro, K. (1978). *Collected poems*. New York: Random House.

Shrodes, C., Finestone, H., & Shugrue, M. (1992). *The conscious reader* (5th ed.). New York: Macmillan.

Sisk, D. (1990). Using the future as an organizing construct for curriculum. *Challenge, 9*(2), 46–50.

Sloan, G. D. (1991). *The child as critic*. New York: Teachers College Press.

Stanford, J. A. (1993). *Connections: A multicultural reader for writers*. Mountain View, CA: Mayfield.

Sullivan, C. (Ed.). (1989). *Imaginary gardens: American poetry and art for young people*. New York: Harry N. Abrams.

Sullivan, C. (Ed.) (1991). *Children of promise: African-American literature and art for young people*. New York: Harry N. Abrams.

Sullivan, C. (Ed.) (1994). *Here is my kingdom: Hispanic-American art for young people*. New York: Harry N. Abrams.

Swann, B., & Krupat, A. (Eds.). (1987). *I tell you now: Autobiographical essays by Native American writers*. Lincoln, NE: University of Nebraska Press.

Swicord, B. (1984). Debating with gifted fifth and sixth graders—Telling it like it was, is, and could be. *Gifted Child Quarterly, 28*, 127–129.

Taba, H. (1962). *Curriculum development: Theory and practice*. New York: Harcourt, Brace & World.

Tchudi, S. (1991). *Planning and assessing the curriculum in English language arts*. Alexandria, VA: Association for Supervision and Curriculum Development.

Thompson, M. C. (1990). *Classics in the classroom*. Monroe, NY: Trillium.

Thompson, M. C. (1990–1991). *The word within the word* (Vols. 1 & 2). Unionville, NY: Trillium.

Thompson, M. C. (1991). *The magic lens: A spiral tour through the human ideas of grammar*. Unionville, NY: Trillium.

Tiedt, I. M. (1989). *Writing: From topic to evaluation*. Boston: Allyn & Bacon.

Toulmin, S., Rieke, R., & Janik, A. (1979). *An introduction to reasoning.* New York: Macmillan.

UNICEF Ontario Development Education Committee. (1988). *Children's literature: Springboard to understanding the developing world.* Canada: Canadian International Development Agency.

Van Devanter, A. C., & Frankenstein, A. V. (1974). *American self-portraits, 1670–1973.* Washington, DC: International Exhibitions Foundation.

VanTassel-Baska, J. (1992). *Planning effective curriculum for gifted learners.* Denver, CO: Love.

VanTassel-Baska, J., Johnson, D. T., & Boyce, L. N. (Eds.). (1996). *Developing verbal talent.* Boston: Allyn & Bacon.

Vetrone, K. (1986). No need to see. *Gifted Child Today, 9*(2), 41–45.

Whitehead, R. (1968). *Children's literature: Strategies of teaching.* Englewood Cliffs, NJ: Prentice-Hall.

Wild, M. (1991). *Let the celebration begin!* New York: Orchard.

Zeitlin, S. J., Kotkin, A. J., & Baker, H. C. (1982). *A celebration of American family folklore.* New York: Pantheon.

Order these outstanding titles by the

CENTER FOR GIFTED EDUCATION

SCIENCE

QTY	TITLE	ISBN	PRICE	TOTAL
	Guide to Teaching a Problem-Based Science Curriculum	0-7872-3328-5	$32.95*	
	Acid, Acid Everywhere	0-7872-2468-5	$32.95*	
	The Chesapeake Bay	0-7872-2518-5	$32.95*	
	Dust Bowl	0-7872-2754-4	$32.95*	
	Electricity City	0-7872-2916-4	$32.95*	
	Hot Rods	0-7872-2813-3	$32.95*	
	No Quick Fix	0-7872-2846-X	$32.95*	
	What a Find!	0-7872-2608-4	$32.95*	

LANGUAGE ARTS

QTY	TITLE	ISBN	PRICE	TOTAL
	Guide to Teaching a Language Arts Curriculum for High-Ability Learners	0-7872-5349-9	$32.95*	
	Autobiographies Teaching Unit	0-7872-5338-3	$28.95*	
	Literature Packets	0-7872-5339-1	$37.00*	
	Journeys and Destinations Teaching Unit	0-7872-5167-4	$28.95*	
	Literature Packets	0-7872-5168-2	$37.00*	
	Literary Reflections Teaching Unit	0-7872-5288-3	$28.95*	
	Literature Packets	0-7872-5289-1	$37.00*	
	The 1940s: A Decade of Change Teaching Unit	0-7872-5344-8	$28.95*	
	Literature Packets	0-7872-5345-6	$37.00*	
	Persuasion Teaching Unit	0-7872-5341-3	$28.95*	
	Literature Packets	0-7872-5342-1	$37.00*	
	Threads of Change in 19th Century American Literature Teaching Unit	0-7872-5347-2	$28.95*	
	Literature Packets	0-7872-5348-0	$37.00*	

Method of payment:

❏ Check enclosed (payable to Kendall/Hunt Publishing Co.)

❏ Charge my credit card:

    ❏ VISA   ❏ Master Card   ❏ AmEx

Credit Card No. _____

Exp. Date _____

Signature _____

Name _____

AL, AZ, CA, CO, FL, GA, IA, IL, IN, KS, KY, LA, MA, MD, MI, MN, NC, NJ, NM, NY, OH, PA, TN, TX, VA, WA, & WI add sales tax.

Add shipping: order total $26-50 = $5; $51-75 = $6; $76-100 = $7; $101-150 - $8; $151 or more = $9

Price is subject to change without notice.   **TOTAL**

Address _____

City/State/ZIP _____

Phone No. (   ) _____

E-mail _____

KENDALL/HUNT PUBLISHING COMPANY
4050 Westmark Drive   P.O. Box 1840   Dubuque, Iowa 52004-1840
A16/mkk Q2 2005 01

Call (800) 228-0810 • Fax (800) 772-9165
Visit us at www.kendallhunt.com

An overview of the outstanding titles available from the

CENTER FOR GIFTED EDUCATION

SCIENCE

A PROBLEM-BASED LEARNING SYSTEM FROM THE CENTER FOR GIFTED EDUCATION FOR YOUR K-8 SCIENCE LEARNERS

The Center for Gifted Education has seven curriculum units containing different real-world situations that face today's society, plus a guide to using the curriculum. The units are geared towards different elementary levels, yet can be adapted for use in all levels of K-8.

The goal of each unit is to allow students to analyze several real-world problems, understand the concept of systems, and conduct scientific experiments. These units also allow students to explore various scientific topics and identify meaningful problems for investigation.

Through these units your students experience the work of real science in applying data-handling skills, analyzing information, evaluating results, and learning to communicate their understanding to others.

LANGUAGE ARTS

A LANGUAGE ARTS CURRICULUM FROM THE CENTER FOR GIFTED EDUCATION FOR YOUR GRADES 2-11

The Center for Gifted Education at the College of William and Mary has developed a series of language arts curriculum units for high-ability learners.

The goals of each unit are to develop students' skills in literature interpretation and analysis, persuasive writing, linguistic competency, and oral communication, as well as to strengthen students' reasoning skills and understanding of the concept of change.

The units engage students in exploring carefully selected, challenging works of literature from various times, cultures, and genres, and encourage students to reflect on the readings through writing and discussion.

The units also provide numerous opportunities for students to explore interdisciplinary connections to language arts and to conduct research around issues relevant to their own lives. A guide to using the curriculum is also available.